SERMONS FROM THE MIRACLES

BOOKS BY THE SAME AUTHOR

SERMONS ON SIMON PETER
MEET THESE MEN
IN PARABLES
THE SEVEN WORDS
ANOINTED TO PREACH
WHEN THE CHURCH WAS YOUNG
QUESTIONS JESUS ASKED
AND THE PROPHETS
CHAPPELL'S SPECIAL-DAY SERMONS
FACES ABOUT THE CROSS
FEMININE FACES
IF I WERE YOUNG
LIVING ZESTFULLY
THE ROAD TO CERTAINTY
SERMONS FROM REVELATION
SERMONS FROM THE PARABLES
SERMONS FROM THE PSALMS
SERMONS ON THE LORD'S PRAYER
THE SERMON ON THE MOUNT
TEN RULES FOR LIVING
VALUES THAT LAST
THE VILLAGE TRAGEDY AND OTHER SERMONS

SERMONS
FROM THE MIRACLES

CLOVIS G. CHAPPELL

ABINGDON PRESS
NEW YORK • NASHVILLE

SERMONS FROM THE MIRACLES

O

SET UP, PRINTED, AND BOUND BY THE PARTHENON PRESS, AT NASHVILLE, TENNESSEE, UNITED STATES OF AMERICA

CONTENTS

I

HIS RADIANT MINISTRY

"God anointed Jesus of Nazareth with the Holy Spirit and with power: who went about doing good, and healing all that were oppressed of the devil; for God was with him."

ACTS 10: 38

THIS IS A PART OF PETER'S SERMON IN THE HOUSE of Cornelius. We are told that this Centurion had been praying, and that God had answered his prayer by telling him where he might obtain a preacher. "Immediately therefore," says Cornelius, "I sent unto thee; and thou hast well done that thou art come. Now therefore are we all here present in the sight of God, to hear all things that are commanded thee of God." Then the Apostle Peter, who had responded to this invitation, under the leadership of the Spirit, delivered his message. At the heart and center of his sermon is our text. It is the very summary of the life of Jesus. It is as beautiful and impressive as it is brief: "God anointed Jesus of Nazareth with the

Holy Spirit and with power: who went about doing good, and healing all that were oppressed of the devil."

I

The first fact that Peter brings before us is the high use that Jesus made of life. What did he do with the privilege of living? He did not use it selfishly, but unselfishly. He went about doing good. He was utterly free from self-seeking. When James and John came to him, asking for special privileges, he declared that he was swayed by no such motives; but, on the contrary, that he had come not to be ministered unto, but to minister. On another occasion he affirmed that it was more blessed to give than to receive. This great truth he had discovered, not by close thinking, but by unselfish living. When we live in any other fashion life loses its tang, its springtime gives place to gloomy winter.

Back in the hill country, where I used to live, there was a standard answer concerning any sick body who was not improving. "How is Mr. Smith this morning?" one neighbor would ask another. "He is not doing any good," would be the sad response. That meant that there were no indications of returning health. Now, those who are not doing any good are always sick. They are missing the gleam to take the gloom. I read of one such not long ago. Living to no purpose, he soured on life. At last, in sheer boredom he decided to end it all. So he made his way to the pier and flung himself into the sea. But he had a friend. That friend had become suspicious, and was watching. So, when he flung himself into the sea, this friend sprang in after him. Now, it so happened that while this would-be suicide was an excellent swimmer, his friend could not swim a stroke. Therefore, when this poor wretch, who was fed up, saw his friend drowning for his sake, he had to help. After a hard struggle, he managed to save him. This experience proved such a thrill that he decided to live. And little by little his boredom vanished through the joy of an effort to do some good in the world.

Now, the fact that Jesus went about doing good indicates not only that he cared, but that he believed that good needed to be done. That is, Jesus recognizes the presence of evil in the world. He was no shallow optimist. He never once ignored the grim tragedy of sin, sickness, and death. He saw with clearer eyes than any other the terrible sufferings of men, their wounds, their bewilderments, their desperation. He saw behind these grim tragedies the deeper tragedy of alienation from God. Jesus faced with clear eyes the grim fact of sin, and all the wretched evils that result from it.

Not only did Jesus face the fact that good needed to be done, but he was convinced that good could be done. That is, he looked on sin as a usurper in God's world. He did not believe it to be a permanent part of the divine plan. Since sin itself was a usurper, so were its tragic consequences. Therefore, Jesus believed that the evils of the world could be cured by getting rid of their cause. It was this faith that made him such a dauntless optimist. The Bible view of sin is often regarded as pessimistic. But it is the only view that offers one ray of hope. For, if sin and its consequences are parts of the natural order of things, then there is nothing to be done about it. But if Christ's view is correct, then we may pray and work in confidence for the coming of the Kingdom. We can look toward the day when the Kingdoms of the world shall become the Kingdoms of our Lord and his Christ.

Now it was in this faith that Jesus went about doing good. He believed in the reality of evil. He believed that man was lost, but he believed that he could be saved. But he believed this was only possible through man's co-operation with God. He never expected either the individual or society to drift into salvation. He believed that if a better world was ever to be made, man was to work with God in the making of it. Gripped by that conviction, he turned his back on his carpenter shop one day to go about doing good, never giving over till they nailed him to the cross. And the way he used his life is the way you and I are to use ours.

II

But, what good did Jesus do? Of course a full answer to this question is impossible. He showed men God. This he did by the life he lived, by the words he spoke, by the deeds he did. It is of his deeds that Peter is especially thinking in our text. He is thinking of the miracles of Jesus, particularly his miracles of healing. The mighty deeds of Jesus were one of the thrilling joys of the early saints. They gloried in them. They saw in them unmistakable evidences that the life of heaven was already beginning here on earth. We do not think of them so joyously. Oftentimes they rather embarrass us. Often we tax our ingenuity in order to explain them away. But in spite of this fact, it is my purpose to speak to you about them for a dozen or more Sundays. This sermon is by way of introduction.

The miracles of Jesus fall roughly into three groups.

1. There are his miracles of healing—miracles that he wrought upon the diseased and maimed bodies of men. As I re-read the Gospels in preparation for this series of sermons, I was astonished at how large a place the ministry of healing had in the brief record of the life of Jesus. He did not heal on rare occasions and grudgingly, as some seem to fancy. He healed lavishly and joyously. He seems to have taken the greatest delight in ministering to suffering bodies. This, of course, is only natural. We can think of few privileges so thrilling as being able to lift some despairing sufferer upon his feet.

Jesus healed those who came to him individually. Matthew tells how, when he came down from the mountain, after his immortal sermon, a leper flung himself at his feet, with this honest prayer: "Lord, if thou wilt, thou canst make me whole." He was sure of the power of Jesus, but he was not quite sure of his love. Life has dealt too harshly with him. The best he could say to Jesus was, "If you choose." And what did Jesus reply to this imperfect faith? He said, "I do choose." And immediately the leper was cleansed. And Jesus was constantly choosing health for those about him, instead of sickness. There was never an instance where he refused to cure because he thought it best for the patient to remain a sufferer.

On another occasion, when Jesus went into the synagogue, he encountered a poor woman who was suffering from a dread disease that had almost bent her double. He at once healed her, and sent her on her way joyfully erect. When the ruler of the synagogue saw her, he was filled with anger. "There are six days in which folks can come to be healed," he declared; "why, then, desecrate the sabbath?" But Jesus turned on him in indignation and said, "You hypocrite, if your ox falls into the pit on the sabbath, you lift him out. And should not this woman, whom Satan has bound all these years, be released on the sabbath?" He regards the woman's infirmity as a part of the kingdom of evil. Therefore, as any good physician would, he fights to set her free.

But not only did Jesus heal when folks came to him individually, but again and again we read of his healing when they are brought to him in groups. Here and there we find such words as these: "And Jesus went about all Galilee, teaching in their synagogues, and preaching the gospel of the kingdom, and healing every sickness and every disease among the people." Then, there is that beautiful picture in Capernaum: "At even, when the sun was set, the whole city was gathered about his door, and he healed them all." Then, in the fourteenth chapter of St. Matthew we read that when he came to Gennesaret the people went into all the country round about and brought to him all that were sick. And he healed them every one. Then, in the fifteenth chapter, we read that great multitudes came unto him, bringing to him the lame and the maimed and the blind. And he healed them all. It is evident, therefore, that Jesus gave a large place to the ministry of healing. And when he sent out his disciples, he told them to heal the sick. And I fear that in our dread of fanaticism we have turned this gracious ministry too largely into the hands of the cults and the faddists.

2. Jesus wrought miracles within the souls of men. There is no argument about this among Christian people. He changed the fluctuating son of Jonah into a rock. He changed John, with his high capacity to hate, into the apostle of love. He found the demoniac of Gerasa, a disintegrated personality, a menace, and made him into a missionary. It was to miracles of spiritual healing that Jesus gave supreme importance.

And we are right in putting the emphasis there still. We know that it is possible for one to be sound physically and rotten spiritually. But we also know that there are many whose physical diseases would vanish like mist before the sunrise if they only found spiritual healing. Then, there are multitudes who are able to suffer bravely and even joyously because they have inward peace. There is no greater miracle than the courage to say in the midst of life's disasters, "We know that all things work together for good to them that love God."

3. Finally, Jesus worked miracles in the realm of nature. These are the ones that the modern man finds it hardest to believe. We read that when Jesus was surrounded by hungry multitudes, he fed them upon resources totally inadequate. On another occasion, when he, with his disciples, was crossing the sea and a sudden storm threatened to wreck his little vessel, his disciples appealed to him for help, even as you and I should have done under similar circumstances. What was the response of Jesus? He did not simply stay the tempests within their hearts and give them courage to see it through with honor. This he will always do when we pray to him aright. This is the best possible. But here he saw fit even to still the sea itself, so that there was a great calm. He believed that it was in the hollow of God's hand that the seas rage and roar, and that they could be hushed at His bidding.

Then, Jesus raised the dead. A dead body is a part of nature. It is a "brother to the clod which the rude swain turns with his share and treads upon." But Jesus did not believe that death was any match for God. When on the way to the house of the ruler of the synagogue he was met by neighbors, telling him that the patient was dead, he did not turn back. "He paid no attention to what they said," is Goodspeed's translation. He went quietly on his way and gave the child back to those who loved her. He was not afraid to have the stone removed from the grave of Lazarus. He knew that there was One present who was mightier than death and that the victory was sure to be with Him. Jesus, then, worked miracles on the bodies of men, within their souls, and within the realm of nature.

III

Not only does the Apostle remind us that Jesus wrought these mighty deeds, but he tells us the power by which he was enabled to work them. He makes it very clear that Jesus did not perform his miracles in the power of his innate deity. When Jesus was born of Mary, he emptied himself. He lived his whole life, not as God, but as man. If Jesus met his temptations and did his mighty works as God, then his incarnation loses most of its meaning for us. Jesus' power was that of a perfect man perfectly filled with the Holy Spirit. So says Peter: "God anointed Jesus of Nazareth with the Holy Spirit and with power: who went about doing good." With him agree all the evangelists.

The power of the Spirit that Jesus realized in its fullness was released in response to the prayer of faith. Where there was no faith, there were no mighty deeds. Where there was no faith, nothing great and thrilling was possible. Where there was faith, everything was possible. Impossibilities could be broken through like so many gossamer threads, and mountains of difficulties could be tossed aside like children's toys. This Jesus declared with his lips, and this he declared also by his deeds. Jesus set no limits to the power of faith. Again and again, when he cures, he attributes the cure to faith.

One day, for instance, when a woman who had been a sufferer for twelve years came to him and touched the hem of his robe, he healed her. When he dismissed her, he said to her this significant word: "Your faith has cured you." When blind Bartimaeus appealed to him for release from his blindness, he restored his sight, and said exactly the same word, "Your faith has cured you." Again, when the Samaritan who, with nine others, had been cured of his leprosy came back and fell down at his feet to give thanks, Jesus sent him on his way with exactly the same word, "Your faith has cured you." As we read the record we are impressed by the fact that nothing seems to have given Jesus greater pain than the lack of faith that he was constantly encountering. We are also made to realize that nothing so thrilled him as the discovery of faith, either in the heart of Jew or Gentile. This was the case because without faith nothing of worth was possible, while with it everything was possible.

But did not Jesus call Lazarus from the dead in the power of his own deity? Did he not say, "Lazarus, come forth"? And have we not heard it emphasized that if he had not specified Lazarus by name, all the dead might have risen? On the contrary, Jesus fairly goes out of his way to tell us that this was not the case. Standing before that grave, he offers a brief prayer of thanksgiving, "Father, I thank thee that thou hast heard me. I know that thou hast heard me always." Jesus won his victory in the secret place of prayer, before he reached that grave. Lazarus was raised from the dead, according to the clear statement of Jesus, in answer to the prayer of faith. And the significant fact is that the resources that Jesus used for the doing of his work are available for every man and woman today who will claim them.

IV

Now, what are we modern Christians living in this scientific age to do with these facts? The Gospels teach, with one voice, that Jesus worked miracles in the power of the Holy Spirit. What does this mean to us?

1. There are those who reject the miracles of Jesus

either wholly or in part. They believe that these stories grew up about Jesus in an unscientific age as stories are prone to grow up about any conspicuously great man. They have the same amount of truth that the story of the cherry tree and the hatchet has regarding Washington. These affirm that miracles cannot happen because nature is a rigid affair, a closed system, where only physical causes can bring about physical effects. They, therefore, dismiss the miracles as at once irrelevant and impossible.

2. Then, there are those who accept the miracles, but accept them only as evidences of the unique deity of Jesus. These declare that Jesus wrought miracles to prove that he was divine, and that, having demonstrated that fact, miracles were no longer useful. Hence they say now that the days of miracles are past. But those taking this position are about as greatly embarrassed as the ones who reject them altogether. This is true, in the first place, because the writers of the New Testament take no such view. Jesus never once worked a miracle just for display. When asked for a sign his answer was, "A wicked and adulterous generation seeketh after a sign." And no such request was ever granted.

This view is embarrassing also because, if the day of miracles is past, it is hard to tell just when it passed. It certainly did not do so at the death of Jesus. If we give credit to the Book of Acts, miracles went right on taking place, not only in the souls of men, but in their bodies, and also in the realm of nature. In the Acts, men were healed of bodily disease. Prison doors were opened, and men facing shipwreck were saved, all in answer to the prayer of faith. But the most embarrassing question of all for those taking this view is, why was this power withdrawn? If the power to do the impossible was needed in the long ago, surely it is not less needed now. If ever the Church was confronted by tasks that call for supernatural power, it is today. And I for one believe that all the power that was available in the time of Jesus is available now.

3. Finally, there are those who accept these miracles substantially as related in the Gospels. They find it easier to do this today than it was three-quarters of a century ago. This is the case because we have learned that nature is not a rigid affair, that it is not a closed system. We have had this fact demonstrated before our eyes again and again. We have discovered, for instance, something of the amazing power that the mind has over the body. We have seen folks stone blind, when there was nothing wrong with their eyes. We have seen deaf folks who had perfect ears, lame folks whose limbs were unimpaired. The trouble with all these was not in their bodies, but in their minds. We know that a hypnotist can put his subject to sleep, press the end of a pencil in his palm, and say, "I am burning you with a red-hot iron." Then he can tie up that hand. Wake the patient, and unwrap it, and there will be a blister burned there, not by a hot iron,

but by the mind. There is no tissue in the body, the *British Journal of Medicine* tells us, that is not influenced by spirit.

Now, if my mind can so influence this physical house in which I live, and there is no measuring how great that influence is, is it too much to believe that the divine mind can influence this physical universe? Jesus did not think so. He believed that the universe was God-made, and that it was plastic in His hands. Such a faith seems to me altogether reasonable. It would seem queer indeed that God would shut Himself up in a universe that He could not control. As I was driving along the road the other day, I saw a sign advertising brakes. It read, "If you cannot stop, don't start." And in all reverence, that would apply to God. If He cannot control His universe, He should not start it. We believe that He can control it. Why did men once say that nature was absolutely rigid? Because they did not know any better. Personally, I believe that the more we learn, the more credible will become the miracles of Jesus.

What, then, does this mean? It means that every human need may be a matter of prayer. It means that we can pray for spiritual blessings, for inner strength, and courage, and peace. It means, also, that while we recognize these as supreme, we can also pray for temporal blessings. We can pray for daily bread, as we do, when we use the prayer that our Lord taught us. It means that absolutely nothing is outside God's interest and God's power. Why, then, is the modern Church so often weak and discouraged and defeated? The answer is plain. It is because it is living beneath its privileges. The vast majority of modern Christians are sub-normal. Wherever any individual or group has become possessed of the simple faith of the early Church, the impossible has become possible, and spiritual winter has been changed into glorious spring. May God give us grace to claim our privileges! And of us, too, it may be written, "God anointed him with the Holy Spirit and with power: and he went about doing good."

Changing Water into Wine

II

THE BEST IS YET TO BE

"Thou hast kept the good wine until now."

JOHN 2: 10

THE TEXT IS PART OF THE STORY OF THE FIRST miracle of our Lord, the turning of water into wine. Indeed, the Apostle does not call this homely service that Jesus wrought a miracle at all. He calls it a sign. "This beginning of his signs did Jesus in Cana of Galilee, and manifested forth his glory." That is, while this kindly deed is important in itself, it owes its chief importance to what it has to teach us regarding our Lord. To the mind of John this sign, in a very profound sense, holds the mirror up to the face of the Master. It reveals something of his character and purpose in the world, also something of his method of achieving that purpose. For this reason it is highly significant to all of us. What are some of the lessons it has to teach?

I

First, it is a revelation of the interest of Jesus in the commonplace. He is interested in ordinary folks and in their ordinary joys and sorrows. The scene is a wedding in an obscure country village. Who is the bride? We do not know. John leaves her nameless. She is evidently some peasant girl whose family has no place in the social register. Who is the bridegroom? He also is nameless—just some ordinary rustic "to fortune and to fame unknown." But when Jesus receives an invitation to the wedding of these commonplace young people, he accepts with gladness. This he does, not condescendingly, nor from a mere sense of duty. He does it rather because he is keenly interested in them; not because of who they are, but because of what they are, human personalities.

Now, what Jesus did here is typical of his conduct throughout his entire ministry. Whenever he received an invitation into anybody's home he accepted it. This he did whether the giver of that invitation was rich or poor, friendly or hostile, socially prominent, or an outcast. That is, he was interested in folks as such. Never once do we find him paying particular attention to any man or woman because of his or her wealth, or rank, or achievement, or intellectual gifts, or social position. He leaves all that for us. He knew too well that "the rank is but the guinea's stamp." But we still bow down to what is outside and accidental. I heard a woman say that she went shopping one day wearing a very ordinary costume; but that the day following she went again wearing her best, and there was a vast difference in the consideration she received. That is, we are interested in certain kinds of folks, but Jesus is interested in just folks.

Now, since Jesus was interested in this bride and groom, all that concerned them concerned him. When, therefore, an embarrassment arose because the bridegroom was too poor to furnish refreshments in sufficient quantity, Jesus threw himself into the breach. This he did, not because wine was an absolute necessity. It was not a matter of life and death. Wine was, however, part of the daily diet of that time. The bridegroom was expected to furnish it, and his failure to do so would have been very embarrassing. It was to save him from such embarrassment that Jesus worked this miracle. During his earthly life he was constantly interesting himself in the ordinary joys and sorrows of the folks about him.

And what he was before he came to the cross, he was after he had risen from the dead. That is a beautiful story that John gives us in the latter part of his Gospel. Peter, with a few of his friends, has returned to his old vocation of fishing. They toil all night, but catch nothing. In the early morning, as they come in from their fruitless labors, they see somebody standing on the shore. At first they do not recognize him. It is the gloaming of the early morning. Then, a question is shouted to them across the waters. It was a question that made their hearts beat quicker: "Lads, have you caught anything?" He is still interested in their interests, just as in the old days. When they tell him of their failure, he tells them how to cast their net so as to be successful.

Then, when a little later they reach the shore, dragging their net full of fish, they find that a fire has already been kindled, and that breakfast is being prepared. "Come and break your fast," he says a moment later. How beautiful it all is! This amazing Christ who has just conquered death and the grave still has time enough and love enough to give himself to the lowly task of preparing breakfast for a little handful of hungry fishermen who have just come in from a fruitless night of toil. And the Christ we see here is the same yesterday, today, and forever. He is the Christ who is interested in our commonplace selves and in our daily joys and sorrows.

II

Second, this is a sign of the purpose of Jesus in the world. What has he come to do? What is he here to accomplish? He is not a thief who is come to steal and to kill and to destroy. He is not come to rob us of our laughter or to cheat us of our joy. He is not come to take one single gleam of sunshine out of our skies. "Pale Galilean, thou hast conquered, and the world has grown gray at thy birth." So sobbed one of the spiritually blind. But a word more utterly false was never uttered. Not only is this untrue; it is the very opposite of the truth.

What, then, is Jesus here to do? He is here to

transfigure and to transform. He gives new glory to everything upon which he lays his hand. He makes the useless into the useful. He lifts the lower into the higher. He makes the colorless water of the worthless blush into the fine red wine of the worthful. He is here to change desert into garden. He is here to transmute the world's moral waste into the world's moral wealth. A man died in the West some years ago named Luther Burbank. Burbank said that every weed was a possible flower. What an amazing confidence he had in his vegetable kingdom! The only reason he thought that that old burweed did not have its hands full of blossoms instead of cockleburs was because no man had cared for its soul.

Now, in proof of the truthfulness of his contention, Burbank undertook the transformation of the cactus. I do not know whether you are personally acquainted with the cactus or not. If you are, you will recognize the fact that it is one of the best armed plants in the vegetable kingdom. It believes in preparedness. You could not slip up on the blind side of a cactus the darkest night that ever came. It is always ready for battle. But Burbank met this unfriendly plant and seemingly fell in love with it. Anyway he gave himself to its training till one day, in a moment of confidence, that cactus responded by putting down all its swords and bayonets, and filling its hands with flowers. When we see it today, we no longer gather our garments about us lest it touch us, but we should like to wear its colorful beauty over our hearts, or rub our cheeks against the soft velvet of its petals. He found what was a positive foe, and made it into a friend.

But the supreme artist in this work of lifting the lower into the higher is none other than Jesus himself. He finds a blundering fisherman named Simon, a creature of impulse, as unstable as water, and makes him into a rock of Christlike character. He finds a thunderbolt named John, capable of such hot hate as to be able to call down fire from heaven on certain misguided villagers who refuse a night's lodging to his Master and himself, and changes him into the Apostle of Love. He finds a grasping tax collector named Matthew and sets him to writing a Gospel. He finds a demon-possessed woman named Mary and makes her the first herald of the Resurrection. He finds an intellectual giant named Paul, the greatest menace of the early Church, and makes him into its greatest missionary. And he is the same Christ still. He still touches every life that will surrender to him, every gift we put into his hands, not to cheapen and to spoil, but to transform and to glorify. He is here to lift the lower into the higher.

III

Then, this is a sign of the method of Jesus.

1. It indicates his method of working his marvelous transformations. How did he change this water into wine? I have no doubt that he could have wrought

the change without any assistance. But he did not see fit to do so. How did he accomplish the task? He did it through the aid of human hands. These servants had to co-operate with him. In fact, they had to do all that they could do before this miracle was made possible. It is ever so. When the hungry multitude is to be fed, he must have the assistance of his disciples. Not only so, but he must lean especially hard upon the shoulders of a nameless laddie who happens to have a bit of lunch in his pocket. When he cures a paralytic and sends him away sound in body and soul, he must have the assistance of four resolute friends who refused to be balked by any difficulties. When he raises Lazarus from the dead, human hands must roll away the stone, and human fingers must loose him and let him go. When the night had settled over Europe, and he wants to bring in the dawning of a new day, he must have the assistance of a Martin Luther. When he would breathe a new spiritual springtime upon a morally dead England, he must have the aid of a hot-hearted Wesley.

In fact, all the transforming work of our Lord waits upon your co-operation and mine. If we would have abundant harvests, he must send the sunshine and the rain, but we must do our part. If we are to have strong physical bodies, we must co-operate with him. A perplexed and worried woman came to see me some time ago to ask me if I thought it would be a sin for her to take the medicine that her physician had prescribed. She had been told that she must leave it all to the Lord. Possibly I misled her, but I advised her to take the medicine. It might be within the power of God to keep me physically strong without my ever eating, but my faith does not work in that direction. I believe that it is my duty to co-operate with Him in eating the right kind of food. I believe, also, it is my duty to co-operate with Him in taking the remedy that the physician prescribes. God's work is not less miraculous because He is assisted by human hands. "I bound up his wounds," said Galen, "and God healed him."

It is my very firm conviction that God wills that we should have a strong and conquering church at the heart of this city. Vigorous churches are needed everywhere, but nowhere, it seems to me, so much as in the downtown sections of the city. A downtown church is to the spiritual life of a city a bit like what the heart is to the human body. If the heart is strong, it pumps the stream of life and power into every part of the body. If it is weak, it weakens the whole body. Even so, if a downtown church becomes weak, it tends to weaken the spiritual life of the whole city. If it is strong, the spiritual life of the city is strengthened. But how are we to have a conquering church? It is up to you and me. God cannot do it alone. The same is true in the world at large. If there is anything to be done in this generation toward the building of a new and better world, we that are alive today are the ones who are going to have to do it. Our Lord has no other way.

2. This is, also, a sign of Christ's method of giving results. When these servants co-operated with him, there was wine and to spare. Our Christ is ever the Christ of abundances. When he wants space, he spreads it out to the point of the infinite. When he wants suns, he kindles them by the million. When he wants stars, he sows them heaven-wide. Even in our little world he does things on a grand scale. When he wants mountains he piles up the Andes and the Alps, the Himalayas and the Rockies. When he wants flowers, he decks the hills and the fields with them. When he wants water, he scoops out the seven seas, and ribbons the world with rivers, and veils the rugged faces of the cliffs with myriad waterfalls.

And if our Lord is lavish in the realm of the physical, he is even more lavish in the realm of grace. When he offers redemption, it is not a scanty gift. "With him is plenteous redemption." When he pardons, he does not do so in a niggardly fashion. "Let the wicked forsake his way, and the unrighteous man his thoughts: and let him return unto the Lord . . . and unto our God, for he will abundantly pardon." When he gives salvation, he purposes to save unto the uttermost. When he promises to answer our prayers, "He is able to do exceeding abundantly above all that we ask or think." When he offers the gift of life, it is not a meager rivulet, it is a brimming river: "I am come that ye might have life, and have it in abundance." When he offers us welcome into his house on the other side, he does not compel us to slip through a mere slit in the door; he gives us an abundant entrance. Thus he is ever the Christ of abundances.

3. This is the sign of Christ's method of meeting our needs. He does so with an ever-increasing satisfaction. He brings life to an ever-growing climax. When the governor of the feast tasted this new wine, he was astonished at its fine quality. "Every man," he said to the bridegroom, in amazement, "every man at the beginning doth set forth good wine; and when men have well drunk, then that which is worse: but thou hast kept the good wine until now." Such a procedure was altogether out of the ordinary. It is so still. The world ever gives its best first. There are many joys that it has to offer, but the thrill grows less and less with the passing of the years. However hopefully we begin the voyage, soon the anchor drags. However brilliant the feast, it soon loses its tang, the wine gives out, and we become wearied. This somber realization sobs its way through some of our best literature. We hear it bitterly from the lips of Byron:

"'Tis not on youth's smooth cheek alone,
The blush that fades so fast,
But the tender bloom of heart is gone
Ere youth itself is past.

O could I feel as once I felt,
And be what I have been,

And weep as I could once have wept,
O'er many a vanished scene,

As springs in deserts found seem sweet,
All brackish though they be,
So midst the withered waste of life
Those tears would flow to me."

We hear it with less of bitterness from the lips of Wordsworth:

"Heaven lies about us in our infancy!
Shades of the prison-house begin to close
Upon the growing Boy;
But He beholds the light, and whence it flows,
He sees it in his joy;
The Youth, who daily farther from the east
Must travel, still is Nature's Priest,
And by the vision splendid
Is on his way attended;
At length the Man perceives it die away,
And fade into the light of common day."

We hear it also plaintively from Hood:

"I remember, I remember
The house where I was born,
The little window where the sun
Came peeping in at morn;
He never came a wink too soon
Nor brought too long a day;
But now, I often wish the night
Had borne my breath away.

I remember, I remember
The fir-trees dark and high;
I used to think their slender tops
Were close against the sky:

It was a childish ignorance,
But now 'tis little joy
To know I'm farther off from Heaven
Than when I was a boy."

How many a weary heart, I wonder, feels with Hood that their life journey is taking them each day a little farther away from heaven? "For the wettest of wet blankets," says Lord Morley, "give me the man who was most enthusiastic in his youth." Another, realizing how life tends to put out the holy fires of our enthusiasm and reduce us to dull and disillusioned plodders, expresses a longing that we might reverse the order of things and begin at the end and work back toward the beginning. That is, instead of being born a baby boy and gradually growing into a disillusioned old man, he longs to be born old, and gradually to grow back to middle life, and from middle life to youth, and from youth to the sweet innocence of childhood. That, of course, is a futile longing. It is utterly impossible of realization, in the first place. But even if it could be realized, it would make of life only a pathetic anticlimax.

But in the fellowship of Jesus we find all for which this man yearned, and far more. With him life is always climbing toward an ever-growing climax. The feast is forever getting better, the tides of joy rising higher. The buds of the heart's springtime are bursting into ever-increasing beauty. For the real Christian, always the best is yet to be. The Golden Age is never of yesterday, but always of tomorrow. "Thou hast kept the good wine until now"—This we shall say at our first meeting with our Master when, with Thomas, we exclaim: "My Lord and my God." "Thou hast kept the good wine until now"—This we shall exclaim as the years come and go, and we get deeper into the intimacies of his friendship. "Thou hast kept the good wine until now"—This we shall say when we awake with his likeness on the other side. "Thou hast kept the good wine until now"—This we shall say as we climb one Alpine height after another with him in eternity. For "we know not what we shall be: but we know that, when he shall appear, we shall be like him; for we shall see him as he is."

Finally, we are to keep in mind how Christ's amazing dream for us is to become a reality. What are we to do that we may assist Jesus in his work of remaking the individual and the world? What are we to do in order to find life better at every step of the way? Mary put the answer into a single sentence: "Whatsoever he saith unto you, do it." Ours is to be a life of surrender, of complete consecration to God. This is the whole of Christianity. It is Christianity in its beginning, Christianity in its course, Christianity in its consummation. If we do this, we shall find that our path shall be, as the path of the just ever is, "as a shining light, that shineth more and more unto the perfect day."

III
ADVENTURING FOR WORLD PEACE

"Nevertheless at thy word I will let down the net."

LUKE 5: 5

PETER IS COMMITTING HIMSELF TO A COURSE THAT he knows will make him look ridiculous in the eyes of every sane fisherman. To cast the nets under the present circumstances is the height of absurdity. But Peter is going to do it because of his confidence in his Master. He does not believe that Jesus will send him on a fool's errand. It is in this high faith that we adventure for world peace. Our Lord has pronounced a blessing upon the peacemakers. Evidently he believes that peace can be made. He expected a good day when men should beat their swords into plowshares and their spears into pruning hooks and learn war no more! Because we share this faith, we dare to adventure for world peace.

I

It is heartening that more people are thinking in terms of world peace today than ever before. This does not mean necessarily that we are better or wiser than our fathers. The tragic experiences through which we have passed have compelled us to think. We have come to our thoughtfulness over roads strewn with human wreckage, wet with human tears, and crimsoned with human blood. We have tested on a larger scale than any other generation just what war is able to accomplish.

A little less than a quarter of a century ago, a small avalanche started in central Europe. This avalanche so increased in momentum and volume that soon two-score nations had been swept into an abysm of blood and tears. We fought on a grand scale. We are far enough away from the tragedy now to realize that while the war promoters were equally wrong, those whose duty it was to fight and die were equally heroic.

You remember the call that came to us from the battlefields of Europe:

"In Flanders fields the poppies blow
Between the crosses, row on row,
That mark our place; and in the sky
The larks, still bravely singing, fly
Scarce heard amid the guns below.
We are the Dead. Short days ago
We lived, felt dawn, saw sunset glow,
Loved and were loved, and now we lie
In Flanders fields.

Take up our quarrel with the foe:
To you from failing hands we throw
The torch; be yours to hold it high.
If ye break faith with us who die

We shall not sleep, though poppies grow
In Flanders fields."[1]

You remember our heroic response:

"Rest ye in peace, ye Flanders dead!
The fight that ye so bravely led
We've taken up. And we will keep
True faith with you who lie asleep,
With each a cross to mark his bed,
And poppies blowing overhead
Where once his own lifeblood ran red!
So let your sleep be sweet and deep
In Flanders fields!

Fear not that you have died for naught,
The torch you threw to us we caught.
Ten million hands will hold it high,
And Freedom's light will never die.
We've learned the lesson that you taught
In Flanders fields!"[2]

If the outcome of this war was disappointing, if our winnings were far too small, it was certainly not due to the smallness of our investment. Too often our best enterprises fail because of our lack of consecration. Too often we bring to our most worthful tasks in church and state efforts that are half-hearted. But such was not the case in our prosecution of the war. Here we gave our best. We gave our newspapers and our magazines. We had to have the press to propagate the multitudinous lies that are so necessary for the prosecution of a modern war. The press must beat

[1] By John McCrea. Used by permission.

[2] By R. W. Lillard.

down the individual mind and change it into a mob mind. In the business of fighting, therefore, lying is just as necessary as bayonets and bullets and deadly poisons. We gave to our task not a few of our pulpits. Some of us preached war as zealously as if our Master had been a military hero. We gave to this undertaking our treasure—all we had, and mortgaged the future. We gave our man power by the million. Our investment was immeasurably great.

From such an investment, we had a right to expect enormous winnings. But here we were doomed to disappointment. When we received our dividend, it consisted of a world-wide economic depression. It consisted of a moral and spiritual depression which was far more terrible and tragic. All our wild dreams of a better day turned to dust and ashes. Entering the war to make the world safe for democracy, we seem to have made it safe for autocracy. More people are living under despotisms at this hour than at any other time in all human history. There are pathetically few real democracies left in the world today. We were fighting to end war, but we seem to have made war all but inevitable.

"But, at least, we won," you answer, in a natural effort at self-defense. But even that is not quite so evident as we thought. A few months ago, Germany marched in and took over the Rhine. When that happened, one of our shrewd militarists declared that Germany had thus won the war; that, therefore, we ought to go over and whip them again. He did not say just why. But of course, the reason is simple. We ought to whip them again in order that they might march back twenty years later and win the war once more. Thus, if any were left alive, we could keep up the vicious circle like a squirrel chasing himself in a cage. But be that as it may, since Germany has taken over the Rhine, the value of our victory does seem a bit more doubtful than we once thought.

There are even those who are convinced that our boasted victory was a liability rather than an asset. Recently Dr. F. W. Norwood, of London, England, startled us by declaring that the entrance of the United States into the war was a genuine calamity. "Had you not entered," he said, "neither side would have won. We would have fought to a muddled draw. Having done so, we would have made peace on a basis of humility and compromise. But by your entrance, you made our victory decisive. Therefore, we made peace, not on a basis of humility and compromise, but of arrogance and pride. We dealt as conquerors with the conquered. Thus we recarved the map of Europe, and made future wars all but inevitable." From all these considerations, it is evident that the greatest war ever fought was a total loss.

II

Since our greatest adventure at war has proved such a failure, many of us have come to mistrust war altogether. It is estimated that only two-fifths of one per cent of our people really want war. Now, the question is, what are the other ninety-nine and three-fifths per cent of us going to do about it? On this question, we divide into various groups.

First, there are those who say that we can do nothing about it. Those who take this position are composed mainly of two groups:

1. They are people without religious faith. They share the pessimism of the preacher of Ecclesiastes. They believe that what has been will be, that the crooked can never be made straight. "Man is a fighting animal," they say. "He fought yesterday, he will fight today, tomorrow, and to the end of the chapter."

2. The other group sharing this pessimistic outlook, strange to say, is made of people who are very religious. One of their number preached on world peace in my pulpit some months ago. He is a man of especially high character and one for whom I have a deep respect. He deplored war as a horrible and hellish thing, but ended by telling us that nothing could be done to prevent it. He declared that the scriptures say that there are to be wars and rumors of wars to the end of the age. Therefore, there is nothing for us to do but to go ahead and kill each other.

Now it seems to me that this is fatalism pure and simple. Surely, it is little short of treason to our Lord and Master. His name was to be called Jesus because he was to save his people from their sins.

Now there is hardly a sin that war does not beget, and make to grow and to multiply. Lying, lust, hate, prejudice, murder—all these and far more are begotten and made strong by war. War is our supreme evil. It is the deadliest foe of mankind. If, therefore, our Lord cannot save us from this sin when we co-operate with him, from what sin can he save us? When he taught us to pray for the coming of his kingdom, he was not teaching us a prayer impossible of realization. But we have little to hope for in the way of world peace at the hands of those who do not believe anything can be done about it.

Second, there are those who hate war, but expect to prevent it by preparedness. Now I am not arguing, at the present, whether we should prepare or not prepare. But what I am saying is this: Preparedness is certainly not the road to peace. Of that we may be absolutely sure. This I say realizing that, though this claim has been made over and over again in such a way as to seem to smack of wisdom, yet in reality, it does not rise to the height of dignified nonsense. To make such a claim is to fly into the face of all history. To make such a claim is fairly to throw dust in the eyes of reason and spit in the face of common sense.

If the way to have peace is to prepare for war, then the way to have educated people is to exile our teachers and destroy our institutions of learning and burn up our libraries. If the way to have peace is to prepare for war, then the way to promote religion is to kill off the ministers and dynamite the churches. If the way to have peace is to prepare for war, then the way to have good health is to wreck our sewage system and disregard all laws of sanitation. If the way to have peace is to prepare for war, then we have learned how to reverse the laws of nature and gather grapes of thorns and figs of thistles. If the way to have peace is to prepare for war, then this is the only realm in all the universe of God where the law of sowing and reaping does not operate.

But the law of sowing and reaping does operate here as elsewhere. What a man sows, he reaps. What a nation sows, it reaps. The nation that is physically prepared for war is also mentally and spiritually prepared. In truth, that mental and spiritual preparation was an absolute necessity before the physical preparation could take place. If, therefore, we prepare the way of Mars, Mars will travel over it. If we prepare the way of the Prince of Peace, the Prince of Peace will travel over it. If that is not true, we are in a world of confusion. How peace will come, we may not know, but of one thing we can be sure, and that is, it is not going to come through battleships and bayonets.

Third, there are those who look for peace for ourselves in America through isolation. In the realization that we are separated from Europe by 3,000 miles of sea, we are going to let Europe and the rest of the world work out their own salvation while we remain safe in our natural isolation. Now, nobody is farther than I from any desire to be involved in another foreign war. If war breaks out in Europe or Asia, I am for the strongest of neutrality laws to keep us from getting involved. Furthermore, if our neutrality is violated, I am for suffering it rather than resorting to war. If, on the way home from this service, a highwayman should approach me and ask me for my dollar, I would give it to him. This I would do, not because of any great desire to be charitable toward him, but because I considered such a course the lesser of two evils. Weaker nations have to suffer the violation of their neutrality. For that very reason, they often fare far better than their strong neighbors. It is better to lose a hundred men than to lose millions.

But while isolation may be helpful, I seriously doubt if it offers the final solution to our problem. This is the case because we are a part of a constantly contracting world. This summer while fishing, I got poison oak on my left ankle. When it began to give me trouble, I remembered a remedy that I used as a boy—carbolic acid. But one important fact I forgot, that was that I used to dilute the acid. Therefore, I put it on straight and rubbed it in with vigor. When that acid began to eat to the bone, there was an insurrection. My hand said, "I am separated widely from this offending ankle, I will have nothing to do with it." My head said, "I certainly had nothing to do with the applying of the remedy, therefore I will have nothing to do with the suffering." But when bedtime came, as well as I remember, we all lay awake together. We are a part of the world, therefore we may count on this: America is either going to help the world make peace, or it is going to help the world make war. It is up to us to choose. The road to peace is not isolation.

Fourth, if the road to peace is not pessimism, not preparedness, not isolation, where shall we find it? I believe it must come out of our building a new world order. It must come through our cultivation of a new spirit of brotherhood. We must really "make" peace. Pacifist is not a winsome word. This is true because to many, a pacifist is one who simply does nothing. But that is not the case. The word pacifist has a "fist" in it, as another has pointed out. It is not a mailed fist, but it is one that requires a far higher courage. We must seek to remove these economic evils that make some nations so desperate as to be willing to fight. The nations that have must be willing to co-operate with those that have not. We must aggressively cultivate a new patriotism.

III

This new patriotism differs markedly from the old.

1. The old patriotism said, "My country, may it always be right; but right or wrong—my country!" The new patriotism says, "My country, may it always be right; but if I am convinced that it is wrong, I will

say so and act accordingly." This will be the case not because this new patriotism means a lesser love. As a pacifist, I concede nothing to the militarist in point of patriotism. As a father, I say, "My son, may he always be right; but my son, right or wrong." That means that I am going to love him whether he is right or wrong, but it does not mean that I am going to aid and abet him when I see him take a course that I believe will end in disaster. I will refuse to do so for love's sake. For love's sake also I will refuse to aid and abet my nation in a course that I believe fatal to its highest interests.

2. The old patriotism was so intense that it made its possessors antagonistic to every other country. The new patriotism enables its possessor to interpret the patriotism of those of another nation through his own. So often, the patriotism of the one hundred percenter, that patriotism that sends us to flout our navy in the eyes of another nation in order to impress them, succeeds only in making enemies. Now, as another has pointed out, a man might as well be an enemy to his country as to make an enemy for his country. That, I think, is self-evident.

A good friend told me this story. He was celebrating Armistice Day in his own church. Out in front was a veritable forest of flags. One of his stewards rushed into the office full of excitement. "A bohunk made a slighting remark about our flag," he said, "and I socked him in the jaw. He is lying out there now."

The preacher, who happened to be a very sane Christian, answered, "I venture that made a patriot of him. I bet the first thing he does when he picks himself up is to crawl to the flag and kiss it." "Now," he said, "let's go out and see if that is not the case." So the preacher and his steward went out together. The man had just picked himself up and was walking a bit groggily down the street. They overtook him and the steward said, "I am sorry I hit you like that." But the man glared and said never a word. "I am sorry I socked you in the jaw," he repeated, but still no answer. Then the preacher broke in. "What my friend is trying to say to you is that he is sorry." But the bohunk was still silent. Then the steward said in disgust, "That's the way with these foreigners; you can't tell them anything." So he went on his way.

But this friend of mine was not satisfied. He ducked into a door till he saw the offender against the flag start for home. He followed him at a safe distance down one street after another till he came to a miserable shack in the slums. When the foreigner had entered this shack, the preacher knocked on the door and was reluctantly admitted. It took him six months, he declared, never seeing him as far apart as two weeks to get into his confidence. Then he told my friend how he was reared in central Europe. He was told that if he would raise $500 he could go to America, the land of brotherhood and opportunity. He slaved for it, then they brought him over in the steerage, kept him a prisoner at Ellis Island, then farmed him out. He said that since his coming he had never had a kind word, and that he came to hate America with all his soul. A few days later, this man asked to be received into the Church. When he had taken the vows, my friend gave him a private vow. "Will you," he asked, "be loyal to America, too?" To which he answered with tears, "I will be loyal to America, too." But a man had just as well be an enemy to his country as to make an enemy for his country.

3. The old patriotism reached its climax by death on the battlefield. This was its highest expression:

> "Theirs not to reason why,
> Theirs not to make reply,
> Theirs but to do and die!"

There was something very heroic in this type of patriotism. But you will notice that the horses on which these cavalrymen rode took the same position as their riders. It was also "Theirs not to reason why," and "Theirs but to do and die!" Surely, the new patriotism calls for something finer than this. It is not only our privilege, but our duty to reason why. If we reason and find that the orders given clash with conscience, then it is our solemn duty to obey God rather than man. But this is the greatest impeachment of the whole military system: It leaves no place for the conscientious objector. In the Gospels we read this significant word: The soldiers crucified Him. Why did the soldiers crucify Him? Because they hated Him? Because they had reached the conclusion that He stood in the path of human progress? No! They crucified Him because their one task was to obey orders. "Theirs not to reason why, theirs not to make reply."

4. Finally, the old patriotism fixed its faith in force. The new patriotism believes there is a greater god than the god of force. About the saddest word, I think, that ever fell from the lips of Jesus was said to his disciples just before the crucifixion. He was under arrest, his friends now saw that he was going to allow himself to be killed. All their big dreams for him were coming to just nothing. Their disappointment was unspeakably bitter. Jesus understood and could hardly endure the heartbreak of it. "Don't you know," he said, trying to save them from the worship of force, "don't you know that I could pray to the Father, and he could send me twelve legions of angels?" But had he thus resorted to force, he might have escaped crucifixion, but he would not have a worshiper in all the world today. He died in the faith that the mightiest power in the world was not physical force, but love and good will.

That high faith must be ours if we expect to win in this great adventure for world peace. We are yet far from the goal, but we are making progress. The nations have passed up more good opportunities to fight in the last five years, I dare say, than in the previous five thousand. Why is this the case? The reasons are partly economical. Some have refrained from war because they were not financially able to fight. But another reason is that in almost every nation today there is a strong minority group of convinced pacifists who are determined at all costs to avoid war. It is these daring souls that are the supreme hope of the world. They are not unmindful of their difficulties. They fling themselves against the clinched fists of stark impossibilities, saying with Peter, "Nevertheless at thy word"—I make the adventure! May their number be increased!

Healing the Man with Palsy

IV

DISTURBING PUBLIC WORSHIP

"And when they could not come nigh unto him for the press, they uncovered the roof where he was: and when they had broken it up, they let down the bed wherein the sick of the palsy lay."

MARK 2: 4

HERE IS A STORY OF A SERVICE THAT WAS INTERrupted. The Preacher was not allowed to finish his sermon. There was a disturbance that made it impossible for him to go on. There are disturbances for which we devoutly thank God. They hearten us and leave us with some of our most bracing and inspiring memories. Many ministers, I am happy to believe, have had disturbances of this kind. But there are others that are very annoying and that leave behind them a sense of defeat and failure. Few, I imagine, even in this enlightened age, have preached for many years without experiencing disturbances of this type.

Some years ago I was preaching to a congregation in a little country village. Quite a goodly company was out, but they heard me on the installment plan. That is, they would come into the house in shifts of twenty or thirty, remain a few minutes, then go out and allow another shift to take their places. But there was one brave woman who remained through the entire service. She had with her two husky boys of about three and five years of age respectively. That she might not be disturbed by them, she had brought along an iron ring for them to play with. I think it had been taken from the hub of a wagon wheel.

Her plan worked with perfect success. The boys gave her no trouble at all. With a loud yell the younger, who sat upon her lap, would throw this ring upon the floor, and let it roll away till it crashed against the wall. With a yet louder yell, the older would fly in pursuit, never stopping till he had recovered it and restored it to his brother. Then they repeated the performance, keeping it up with unflagging zeal till the service was over. I do not think anything I said in my sermon registered. I hope, however, that my patience made a lasting impression.

But, I confess that I have not always done so well. My patience at other times has not been so much in evidence. On a few occasions, in fact, especially when big babies were doing the disturbing, I have allowed myself to get all hot on the inside, if not without. I have also known other ministers far better than myself to do the same. A few years ago an exceptionally able and consecrated evangelist was preaching to a great congregation in one of our Southern cities. Near the front was an old gentleman who coughed and wheezed and cleared his throat in a manner that was most distressing. At last the preacher seemed completely to lose his temper. He rebuked the disturber in no uncertain fashion. But the outcome was not happy. The preacher soon realized that by losing his temper he had also lost his congregation.

But if there are disturbances that are vastly annoying, there are others that are very thrilling. Such a one occurred when Peter was preaching in the house of Cornelius. The Apostle was delivering an excellent sermon, one into which he was putting his whole heart. But just when he was coming to his climax, just as he was telling how salvation was for everybody on the simple condition of faith, he was interrupted. "To him give all the prophets witness, that through his name whosoever believeth in him shall receive remission of sins." That was as far as the preacher got. He was then shouted down. "While Peter yet spake, the Holy Spirit fell on all them that heard the Word." But Peter was not annoyed. He even remembered that interruption with unspeakable gratitude and joy.

That was a magnificent interruption that occurred when Charles G. Finney was preaching in a certain city in the State of New York. Far back in the balcony sat the Chief Justice of the Supreme Court of that State. As this able lawyer listened to the preacher, he said to himself, "What he is saying is true. Since it is true, I ought to act upon it. Since I ought to act upon it, I ought to do so now." Therefore, he arose, made his way out of the balcony, down the long aisle of that crowded church, and up into the pulpit. Plucking Mr. Finney by the sleeve, he said, "If you will call for decisions for Christ now, I am ready to come." Mr. Finney did not get to finish his sermon, but he did not grieve over being thus disturbed. He rather thanked God. Now it was an interruption somewhat like this of which we read in our text.

I

Look at the story. The scene is a certain house in the city of Capernaum. Just what house this was it is impossible to say. Some think it was the house of Simon Peter, where the Lord was a guest. Others think that it was the house of the Master himself, since he was living in Capernaum at that time. David Smith argues that it was the synagogue. Now, since there were scribes and doctors of the law present from all over the country, even from places as far away as Jerusalem, this view seems the most reasonable. So many notables could hardly have been accommodated in a house as small as that of Jesus or of Simon, even if no others had been present. But there were many besides these. Therefore, it is safe to conclude that this was a week-day service in the synagogue.

The congregation on that day was unusually large. The atmosphere was tense and expectant. Some of these people were heart-hungry. They were there because they were in need of help. There were others who were merely curious. They saw a great crowd of people thronging into the church, and that awakened their interest. Nothing draws a crowd like a crowd. "Something out of the ordinary must be going on," they said to themselves. And at once they determined to find out what that something was. Then, there were others still, including these scribes and doctors, that were present in the role of critics. They were bent on catching some word from the Preacher that would discredit him. All these made a large and eager audience.

The Preacher was holding the fascinated attention of his hearers. He was always vastly interesting. This was the case for many reasons. He was interesting, in the first place, because he was interested. That is, those that heard him felt that he cared. He was interesting, also, because he talked to people about their fundamental needs. Then, he was interesting because he spoke a language that all could understand. The masses always heard him gladly. But he realized before he finished this sermon that he was losing the attention of his audience. Their eyes began to stray from his face to the ceiling where queer noises could be heard. Particles of dust and plaster began to drop, some even falling upon the dignified heads of the doctors of the law. Then, a queer object came floating down from above, to rest on the floor at the Master's feet. It was a bed upon which lay a wreck of a man who was so motionless that he seemed utterly dead except for his haunted and wistful eyes. At this, the Master's sermon came to an abrupt end.

II

Who was responsible for this disturbance? Of course we know that more than one was implicated. There were five. But, I am confident that there was one ringleader upon whose shoulders rested most of the responsibility. This was a man who had doubtless met Jesus before. He had come to know him, to believe in him, to love him. Having found the Master for himself, he began at once to think of a friend of his who was sorely afflicted. He had perhaps known this friend for years. He had caroused with him during a misspent youth. Having a strong constitution, he had weathered those years of riotous living without becoming a wreck. But it was not so with his friend. He was now paralyzed. In utter helplessness, he was compelled to face a past that was a blot, a present that was a blank, and a future that was a nightmare. Naturally this man who was whole was eager to bring his afflicted friend to Jesus.

His first step in that direction was to secure the consent of this friend, to arouse in him hope and confidence. Having succeeded in this, he next enlisted three others who were to help. Perhaps they had all been boon companions in their younger years. They talked things over as they sat beside the sick friend and perfected their plans. Jesus was out of the city at the time, but they decided that immediately upon his return they would certainly bring their afflicted friend into his presence. Then, one day the news was flashed about the city that the Master had returned. These four went at once to the house of their unfortunate friend. The whole committee was present. That speaks well for them. Not one of them had something more important to do. Each man took his corner of the mat and away they went on their mission for healing.

But when they reached the church, they ran into difficulties. They found such a mob within and without as to make any approach to the Master through the door an impossibility. Some doubtless were for taking the poor fellow back home and coming another day. But this leader would not hear of it. He was resolute. He was determined to see the matter through then and there. "Lay him down a minute," he said, "while I look the situation over." He glances here and there and discovers a stairway leading up the outside of the church. He bounds up these stairs two steps at a time. He pauses at the top, looks the situation over, and hurries back with sparkling eyes.

"Take hold," he says, "and let's go." They mount the stairs, and again lay down their burden. Then the leader begins tearing up the roof. "It is against the law," says one. "Never mind," is the answer, "we have got to get this man to Jesus." And soon all four are working away at it. When the opening is large enough, the four of them take their sashes and each ties his to a corner of the bed. Then they lower it through the ceiling until their friend is right at the Master's feet. Then, without a word they lay prone upon their faces and watch to see what the Master will do.

Now, this is as far as they can go. They have done all that is humanly possible toward the helping of their friend. Maybe nothing will come of it all. Maybe, when the services are over, they will have to pick up their pathetic burden and trudge home again with their friend not one whit better, but just a little more wretched and a little more hopeless. But if such should be the case this at least will be true, the fault will not be theirs. What happens, now that they have done their best, is up to the Master. If there is failure, if it all ends in grim tragedy, it will not be their failure, but his.

III

Now, what actually does happen? Is Jesus impatient because he has not been allowed to finish his sermon? Not in the least. I think he is greatly rejoiced. Mark tells us of the reaction of Jesus in these words: "When Jesus saw." What did he see?

1. He saw past what was outward in this sufferer

and his friends to what was inward and fundamental. He saw their beautiful eagerness to get the sufferer into his presence. But he saw something more fundamental than that. He saw the high courage that enabled them to do this daring and unconventional thing. But he saw something that was deeper and more important than that. He saw their patient and dogged persistence that refused to be balked by difficulties. But he saw something even finer than that. He saw what lay behind all these, what made all these possible. He saw their faith. It was their deep conviction of the power and willingness of Jesus to help that made them so earnest and courageous and persistent.

2. Not only did Jesus see their faith, but he also saw the supreme need of the sufferer. What was the matter with this man? He was paralyzed. Anybody could see that. He could not move a muscle. But his paralysis was only a symptom of an inner disease. While I was pastor in Washington I was rather a zealous tennis player. But my tennis arm got to paining me so badly that I feared I would have to give up the game. I made up my mind to consult a physician. Desiring the best possible, I picked out the physician to the President of the United States. Having put me through a careful examination, he gave me relief, and I have never had any trouble with my arm since. How was this cure wrought? He did not cure me by treating my arm. He did not have me to rub it with a certain liniment, or to put it into a sling.

But what he did was to remove my tonsils. That is, instead of treating the symptoms, he treated the disease.

This was the method of Jesus. He always saw into the heart of things. As he looked into the wistful face of this sufferer, he saw there a deeper tragedy than mere physical helplessness. He saw the tragedy of sin. There were outward consequences of this man's wayward life that all eyes could see, but there were inner consequences known only to the sufferer himself and to the tender Christ who was now bending over him. This man was suffering in his body, but he was suffering yet more in his mind. As he lay there, his very helplessness and wretchedness were pleading with the Master and saying:

> "Canst thou not minister to a mind diseased,
> Pluck from the memory a rooted sorrow,
> Raze out the written troubles of the brain,
> And with some sweet oblivious antidote
> Cleanse the stuffed bosom from that perilous stuff
> Which weighs upon the heart?"

And Jesus answered that inarticulate prayer by saying, "My son, thy sins are forgiven thee."

Now, when Jesus said that he spoke home to the deepest needs, not only of this man, but of every man. This is true because of what forgiveness involves. Forgiveness is not merely the remission of a penalty. Forgiveness means the restoration of a broken fellowship. It means that we trust God, and that He trusts us, that He takes us back into His confidence, and forgets that we have ever sinned. It means a new nature. It means that God comes to possess us, and we come to possess Him. Therefore, if we have forgiveness and nothing else, we are still unspeakably rich, because we have God. On the other hand, if we possess all else and miss forgiveness, we are unspeakably poor, because we are without God and without hope.

Not only did Jesus forgive this man, but he saved him from the consequences of his sin. This he did by healing his body. Of course there are certain types of physical disease for which forgiveness is an effective cure. This is true of all those diseases that are the result of an inward conflict, of a quarrel of the soul with God. There are people, for instance, whose minds are so poisoned by hate that they are sick in body as well as sick in soul. I have in mind now one who, I am sure, is a case of this kind. She is unspeakably miserable. Her physical health is wretched. All the strength she has seems to spend itself in intense hatred. Now, if she would only accept the forgiveness of God and thus learn to forgive, the chances are that she would be healed in body as well as in mind. At least, such has been the case with many another.

But generally speaking, forgiveness does not save us from the consequences of our sin. David was forgiven, but in spite of that fact the sword of tragedy continued to pursue him to the very end. I was called to see a woman some time ago who was slowly dying of a poison that was self-administered. During her long hours of suffering she had been made to think. Thus thinking, she had become sorry for her deed. As we talked together, she turned her pain-pinched face toward mine and asked if I thought God would forgive her. I told her that I was sure of it. Then I was privileged to preach the gospel to her. Not only so, but I became confident that she had accepted the forgiveness that Jesus was so eager to give. But one thing that forgiveness did not do for her—it did not take away the poison that was slowly destroying her life.

But here Jesus did the unusual. He not only said, "Thy sins are forgiven thee"; he also said, "Arise, and take up thy bed, and walk." And immediately the sufferer was healed in body as he had been healed in soul. How did Jesus come to perform this lesser miracle? On the surface it seems to have been wrought in answer to the doubts of the doctors of the law who were accusing Jesus of speaking blasphemy when he claimed power on earth to forgive sin. But such is not the case. Of course Jesus claimed the right to forgive. He not only claimed it, but proved it here, and countless millions of times. But this man was healed in body as he was healed in soul, not in response to doubt, but in response to faith. To those who merely seek a sign, no sign is ever given. But to those who believe, all things become possible.

Now, the Jesus about whom this crowd gathered

in Capernaum long ago is with us still. He still has power on earth to forgive sin. Maybe you have a friend who needs him. Maybe there is one dearer to you than life who is desperately in need of one who can save. Why not use the wisdom of these four friends? Bring him to Jesus. He will not disappoint you, as he did not disappoint them. Maybe the sufferer is none other than yourself. Maybe you are experiencing even now the restlessness and wretchedness of separation from God. If so, it need not be the case a moment longer. There is one present who is eager to say to you, "Courage, my child, thy sins are forgiven thee." Just accept that forgiveness, and you will go away singing with the saints of yesterday:

"My God is reconciled,
His pardoning voice I hear;
He owns me for His child,
I can no longer fear:
With confidence I now draw nigh,
And 'Father, Abba, Father,' cry."

Healing the Paralytic
by the Pool of Bethesda

V

THE WHINER

"Sir, I have no man, when the water is troubled, to put me into the pool: but while I am coming, another steppeth down before me."

JOHN 5: 7

HERE IS A STORY THAT WILL LIVE FOREVER. IT will live because it is so genuinely human and so refreshingly hopeful. The scene is one of the porches at the pool of Bethesda in Jerusalem. It is a Sabbath day and the city is thronged with worshipers that have come up to the feast. Many are now passing through these porches on their way to the temple. All about them is a depressing company of sick and blind, lame and hopeless. But these eager worshipers do not see them. They are too busy, or too selfish, or too cowardly. They are far too absorbed in their religious duties to take knowledge of this broken earthenware that the world of their day has ruthlessly tossed aside.

But there is One among them who is beautifully different. He has an eye for those who have fallen behind the procession. Therefore, he comes of set purpose to this cinderpile, this human dumping ground, and picks out the man for whom the world has least hope and who has least hope for himself. This man has lain here thirty-eight years. For half a lifetime, he has waited for something to happen that has never taken place. Now, thirty-eight years is a long time in any man's life. It is a long time for one whose hands are busy with great and thrilling tasks. It is doubly long for one whose hands are weak and empty. It is all but interminable for one who is sick, without friends and without hope. Such is this paralyzed man to whom Jesus comes.

There had been a time when he had stood upon his feet as other men. Possibly, he had been the leader of a group of boon companions. Jesus indicates, you remember, that his present plight is the result of his own wrongdoing. "Behold, thou art made whole," the Master warns; "sin no more, lest a worse thing come unto thee." No doubt when his sickness first came upon him, these friends were shocked and grieved. They came to see him. They sent him flowers. But he neither died nor got well. Therefore, their visits grew less and less frequent, their offerings of flowers dwindled to nothing. One by one, his old friends moved away, or died, or forgot. He made no new friends. Thus, after thirty-eight years he is hopeless and alone.

But on this day of days, he finds himself face to

face with a new experience. He is being searched by the most kindly eyes into which he has ever looked. He does not know who Jesus is. Perhaps he has never even heard of this amazing Prophet who is causing so great a stir among the people. But while he is wondering, this winsome Stranger asks him a question. It is a queer seeming question. "Wilt thou be made whole?" he asks. "Would you like to get well?" "Would you like to stand on your feet and play a man's part in the world?"

I

What did Jesus mean by this queer question? What is implied in it?

1. Jesus is facing with this man the fact of his sickness. He is meeting him on his own ground. He is seeking the man's confidence by telling him that he knows what the invalid knows about himself. When he asks, therefore, "Wilt thou be made whole?" he is saying, "I know that you are sick. I know just how harshly life has treated you. You are not shamming. You have not lain here all these years with nothing the matter. You know and I know that there is something wrong." Jesus knows that he will have little hope of helping this man unless he faces with him the fact that he is sick and in need of help.

Now the question that Jesus puts to this man is intensely individual and personal. It is also universal. He asked it 1900 years ago; he asks it today. He asks it of you and of me, of all of us. Perhaps there are those who resent this question because it implies that they are morally sick. But resent it how you may, the fact remains that our gospel is a gospel for sinners and for sinners only. Jesus declares emphatically that he has not "come to call the righteous." If, therefore, you are all that you ought to be, then his message of salvation has no meaning for you.

But when we face the facts about ourselves, we know that we are not whole. Paul's declaration that all have sinned may leave some of us a bit cold. But as he goes on to add that we have come short, we know that he is telling what is true of all of us. We are not crooks. We are not gangsters. We are neither rakes nor libertines. But, in spite of the fact that we are as decent as decency, we know that we are not living as abundantly as we ought. We have come short. We are not whole. It is the candor of Jesus in telling us this that is his first step toward winning our confidence.

2. Not only does Jesus imply the reality of this man's sickness, but also the possibility of his cure. There is hope in the question. There is the expectation of the dawn of a better tomorrow. If this is not the case, then Jesus is guilty of sheer cruelty. Suppose after saying to a hungry man at my door, "Would you like a good dinner?" I should hasten to shut the door in his face; would I not be cruel? Suppose I should give hope to a drowning man by asking, "Would you

like to be saved?" and then refuse to help him; would that be kind? Did you ever see a boy hold a piece of bread just out of reach of a hungry dog, have the poor fellow jump for it till he tired, and then end by eating it himself? It is a thoughtless and cruel procedure. We resent such treatment, even toward a dog. Surely, therefore, the tender Christ will not tantalize this poor wretch by a dream of wholeness when he knows his dream is impossible of realization.

Now since this question implies the possibility of wholeness for this man of the long ago, it implies no less for you and me. Jesus is always seeing possibilities in us that no one else sees. He is a Christ of infinite hope. He believes that fluctuating Simon may become a rock. He believes that narrow, sectarian John may become a prophet of love. He believes that gloomy Thomas may become spiritually radiant. He is also certain that we can live more richly, more courageously, and more helpfully than we are living. "However you may have failed up to this hour," he is saying, "you need not continue to fail. You may yet do something far bigger and better than what you have done. However mean and lean your life may have been, you may yet find your place at the feast of the fullness of life."

3. Then this question implies that if the man is made whole he must put himself unreservedly in the hands of his Questioner. Should a modern physician say to one who was ill, "Would you like to get well?" his question would imply, not only that the man was

sick, not only that the physician saw a possibility of recovery, but that, in order to realize that recovery, the patient must put himself fully into the hands of his physician. "You are sick," Jesus is saying to this man, "but there is a chance for your recovery. That chance can only be realized by your following my directions. If you give yourself in wholehearted obedience to me, then your recovery is sure. If you do not, I can do nothing for you."

And this word is just as pertinent for you and me as it was for this paralytic. If we are to find individual wholeness, we must find it at the hands of Jesus. If we are to come to possess the fullness of life, we must receive it from him. He is come that we might have life and have it in abundance. If we are to build a strong and victorious church, we must build it in obedience to him. If we are to find social salvation, he is our hope. If we are to build a new and better world, we must build it under his leadership. "There is none other name under heaven given among men whereby we must be saved."

4. This question implies, finally, that if this man is to receive the wholeness that Jesus is eager to give, he must be willing to receive it. Our Lord will not and cannot give what we are unwilling to receive. The same is true of ourselves. However eager you may be to give your boy an education, you cannot give it to him if he will not take it. You cannot give even so trifling a treasure as a coin to any man who will not

receive it. Jesus, therefore, is saying to this paralytic, "You are sick. You can be made whole. If you put yourself in my hands, I am both willing and able to cure you, but I cannot cure you against your will. I can only stand at the door and knock. Weak as you are, you can keep me shut out of your life, if you want to. But if you are willing, I can meet your needs."

Since this is the case, if this man continues prone upon his back, missing all that makes life worth living, it will be his own fault. He will have none to blame but himself. The Church has been careless of him, his friends have forsaken him, but that need not prove fatal. The only disaster that can spell utter ruin is his refusal to take what Jesus so freely offers. That is the only disaster that can work your ruin and mine. He is here offering you healing—he is doing far more, he is offering you the all-inclusive gift of himself. His word is "receive ye." We do not have to wrench his gift from clinging and unwilling fingers. All he asks of us is our willingness to receive.

II

Now, what reply does this man make to this question that is so full of hope? Listen! "Sir, I have no man, when the water is troubled, to put me into the pool: but while I am coming, another steppeth down before me." That is, he accepts readily the implications of Jesus that he is sick, but that is as far as he is willing to go. He does not confess the slightest expectation of recovery. I am persuaded that his long dead hopes are beginning to stir with some slight promise of a resurrection, but he is not yet willing to acknowledge this. He is further still from accepting any responsibility for either being or remaining what he is. Instead, he seems to say, "I can never be whole. But it is not my fault. This is the case for two reasons: First, I am not able to attain wholeness in my own strength. Second, I have nobody to help me. It is every fellow for himself and the devil take the hindmost. Therefore, as a sick man in a sick social order, there is nothing for me but despair."

Now, this is a mood that is all too prevalent today. It is a heartening fact that so many people are keenly sensitive to the desperate needs of our present world. We realize as never before the cruel inequalities born of wrong economical conditions. We are alive to the insanity of war as no other generation has been. We grieve over the weakness of the church. We deplore race prejudice and the wide chasms that divide nation from nation. But too often we are so conscious of our own personal needs and of the appalling greatness of the task that we are stricken with paralysis. Having failed to find inward peace, we despair of bringing about peace throughout our troubled world.

III

Now, what does Jesus say to this man who has despaired both of himself and of his fellows? He calls him to the facing of his own personal responsibilities. Of course no man can preach an adequate gospel who deals solely with the individual. Our gospel is both social and individual. But there is a way of preaching the social gospel that merely leaves the individual with a sense of bewilderment and helplessness. Having heard of appalling world conditions, he asks himself, "What can I do about it?" And the answer oftentimes is, "Nothing." But such answer is always wrong. When a hunter flushes a covey of birds, he does not let the fact that he cannot kill them all prevent his shooting at any of them. He singles out one bird and tries to bring him down.

This is the equivalent of what Jesus says to this man. He tells him to begin with himself. That is always a right starting point. The first duty of every reformer is to reform himself. The first duty of everyone that would give life is to find life for himself. We shall do little toward saving a whole world unless we have done something toward saving ourselves. Therefore, Jesus gives this man a threefold command. It is personal and individual: "Rise, take up thy bed, and walk." It is also logical, as another has pointed out. We must keep the divine order. It is not, "Walk, take up thy bed, and rise." Before we are ready to walk, we must get on our feet. A good many forget this. But the man who undertakes to walk when he is flat of his back can do nothing but kick. Most of the kickers that worry us are folks who never dare to get upon their feet. Look now at these commands in their order.

1. "Rise!" While this whiner is telling the Master how impossible it is for him to be made whole, Jesus speaks to him this word of authority, "Get up!" That seems a strange command. That is the very thing that this paralytic cannot do. Jesus is, therefore, challenging him with the impossible. But this is his method always. We are prone to excuse ourselves for the sins and shortcomings that have an unusually tight grip on us. We say, "That is my peculiarity—that is my weakness." But Jesus is not come to save us from the sins from which we can save ourselves. He is come to enable us to do the impossible.

One day, for instance, he went into the temple and found a man with a withered hand. He said to him, "Stretch forth thy hand." That was the very thing that the unfortunate man could not do. Yet, as he undertook it, the impossible became possible. He is constantly calling us to these big impossibilities. He is calling us to be born anew. He is calling us to love, not only the decent and kindly folks that love us, but to love our enemies as well. He is calling us to be the salt of the earth, to make disciples of all nations, to establish the kingdom of God in a world. His call is constantly to the impossible. What happened when He commanded this prostrate man to get on his feet? Even while he was telling Jesus how utterly hopeless his case was, he was doing what Jesus had commanded.

How did it come about? He simply willed what Jesus willed for him. When a man does that, all of the energies of God become available for him.

2. Having gotten this man upon his feet, the next command of Jesus is, "Take up thy bed." Why did he tell the healed man to do that? Is he urging him to save this worthless old mat that has served him for so long? No. He is still trying to save the man. He told him to take up his bed, according to Dr. Marcus Dods, to keep him from making any provision for a relapse. I think that is a wise word. Suppose this healed man had said to himself, "I am cured, it is true, but there is no telling how long I am going to stay that way. My weak knees are liable to buckle under me before I have gone half a block. Therefore, I will just leave my mat here so that I may have a resting place, in case of failure." Had he taken that course, he would have been flat on his back within the next thirty minutes.

"Take up thy bed" is the wise command of Jesus. That is, make no provision for returning to the old life; burn your bridges behind you. I used to have a friend who had a persistent habit of quitting tobacco. It would be impossible to tell how many times he swore off from the use of the weed. But whenever his wife would go through his pockets, she would almost invariably come upon a half plug of tobacco. When she questioned him about it, he had a standing answer. "I am not carrying that with me to chew, but only to smell." Naturally, he was constantly falling back into his old habit. Some time ago, I was talking to a young man who had come forward in token of the fact that he was going to be a Christian. I asked him to unite with the Church. But he refused. He said, "I intend to join the Church sometime, but not now. I want to see if I can hold out before I take that final step." When he said that, I knew that he was not simply going to backslide, but that he had already backslidden. The only way to live a new life is to make a clean break with the old.

3. The final command of Jesus is, "Walk." You have been carried long enough. You have been out of the game long enough. You have whined about your own weakness, about the faults of the Church, about the rottenness of society, long enough. Try carrying your part of the load. If things are not what they ought to be, then get up on your own feet and help to make them better. Bernard Shaw gives a rather refreshing definition of a gentleman. "A gentleman," he says, "is one that puts more into life than he take out of it." And Jesus is calling this man to be a gentleman. "Rise, take up thy bed, and walk." Begin here and now to face up to your own personal responsibility. Set yourself today, this moment, to doing what you believe God would have you do. To take this course is surely to find life and victory.

Some twenty-five centuries ago there was a brilliant young man who was all but overwhelmed by his own desperate needs and by the appalling needs of his people. "Woe is me," he sobbed bitterly, "woe is me. I am undone. I am a man of unclean lips and dwell in the midst of a people of unclean lips." But if this man had stopped there, his name would have perished long ago. But he found personal cleansing. Then as he heard the voice of God saying, "Whom shall I send, and who will go for us?" he dared to answer, "Here am I; send me!" Thus, Isaiah not only found peace, but he made the whole world richer because of his full and courageous life. And this is the way out for you and me. We are to begin, as Carlyle said, by doing the duty that lies closest to us. If we dare to do this, our victory is sure. "Wouldst thou be made whole?" Begin now to follow him. "Rise, take up thy bed, and walk."

Healing the Man with the Withered Hand

VI
HOW TO GET ANGRY

"He looked round about on them with anger."

MARK 3: 5

UPON ENTERING THE SYNAGOGUE ON THIS OCCAsion, Jesus found himself face to face with a man with a withered hand. Luke tells us that his right hand was withered. He was, therefore, a man with a handicap. He was forced to meet the demands of life at a disadvantage. He represented that great class of hampered and underprivileged people that ever made a strong appeal to the heart of Jesus. The people standing about were naturally on tiptoe of expectancy. They knew that, now that a man with a need was standing face to face with Jesus, something wonderful was likely to happen. Their faces, I can well imagine, were all aglow with eager interest.

But there were those present to whom this expectancy brought no glow of soul. They viewed the scene with hard eyes and sour faces. These were the Pharisees. They were there as the custodians of the law. They felt that it was their business to see to it that this young Carpenter did not desecrate the Sabbath. By their very attitude they were saying to Jesus, "Don't you dare heal this man on the Sabbath day. If you do, it will be an affront to us who are the religious leaders of the people. You will fly in our faces, who are the people of power, and we will never forgive you."

Naturally Jesus, with his fine sensitiveness, was conscious of their opposition. Having invited the man whom he was to heal to stand forth, he asked them a question, "Is it lawful to do right on the Sabbath, or to do wrong? to save life, or to kill?" That was a simple question, and they knew the answer. But they maintained a stony silence. Then it was that Jesus looked round about upon them with anger, being grieved at the hardness of their heart. Then with flaming eyes and glowing cheeks, he bade the man to stretch forth his hand. And as he willed to do what Jesus willed for him, the impossible became possible, and he was cured.

I can see the light of a great joy break over his face. But there is no light upon the faces of these religious leaders. Instead, as Luke tells us, they were filled with fury. In hot anger they went from the synagogue with their minds made up that they would never rest till this man, who cared so much more for personalities than he cared for institutions, was destroyed. But as angry as they were, I dare say they were not one whit more angry than Jesus, who had wrought this miracle of healing.

I

Now the fact that Jesus, the tender and loving Christ, got angry is to some a bit bewildering. This is true because anger is not generally regarded as a virtue, but as a vice. It is so often a mark of littleness rather than of bigness. No greatness of intellect is required to get angry. The most stupid can do it quite as well as those that are wise. It is an achievement that is as readily within reach of the young as of the old. We have all seen babies far too young to talk, but never one too young to lose his temper, and become blood-red with rage.

Since this is the case, it is not surprising that the Bible does not encourage anger. The author of the thirty-seventh Psalm, for instance, bids us "cease from anger, and forsake wrath." "Don't fret in any way," he urged, "because it tends only to evil." Then another psalmist whom Paul quotes with approval writes, "Be angry and sin not." That is, he permits anger, but recognizes the fact that it is a close neighbor to sin, that the man who is angry is more likely to do some ugly wrong than one who is not. And the writer of the Proverbs has this wise word: "He that is slow to anger is better than the mighty." To fly off the handle, to go into a rage, he feels is a mark of weakness, while to control one's temper is a mark of strength. And with this wise man we agree.

When we turn to the New Testament we find the same attitude of disapproval. "Put away anger," Paul writes to his converts at Colosse. In his immortal ode to Love, he tells us that love is sweet-tempered. In his letter to Titus, when he speaks of the qualifications for a bishop, he says that he must not be hot-tempered. We can all see the wisdom of that. A bishop has considerable power over his brethren. Therefore one is not to be trusted with this high office unless he is able to control his temper.

But it remains for Jesus to say the sharpest and most convincing word. "Ye have heard," he says, "that it was said by them of old time, Thou shall not kill; and whosoever shall kill shall be in danger of the judgment: but I say unto you, That whosoever is angry with his brother shall be in danger of the judgment." The law only forbade striking the deadly blow. Jesus went back of all that to the deadly passion that prompts the blow—the passion of anger. "Anger," he says, "is incipient murder." No wonder, then, that Jesus warns against it.

Now since the Bible thus discourages anger, we naturally look upon it with suspicion. Folks that readily lose their tempers, we cannot regard as well-developed Christians. Some time ago a certain preacher was disturbed while he was doing his best to deliver his sermon. The disturbance was annoying. But the saddest part of the whole unfortunate affair was that the preacher lost his temper, made himself quite ridiculous, and sent many of his congregation away, seriously discounting his Christianity. And more than one minister has fallen into this slippery pit. Right or wrong, we tend to question the genuineness of those Christians who cannot control their tempers.

Some time ago a minister told me this story. He had in his congregation a woman who was very active and effective. But her husband, though a good man, did not identify himself with the Church. One day this minister went to him and pressed him for a reason. They were close friends, and at last, in confidence, he gave his reason. "My wife," he said, "is a good woman and one of the best workers you have in your church, but she has a perfectly hellish temper. Now and then she goes into a rage and the children and I simply have to hide out. This," he said, "is not my idea of what it means to be a Christian."

Now this preacher was a brave man. He went away from this interview to another with the wife. He told her frankly what her husband had said. By a desperate effort she controlled her temper. Then she and the minister knelt in prayer. A few days later that husband was going fishing. He came into the house with his fishing rod on his shoulder, and in turning about he touched a new swinging lamp that had just been put up. It fell with a crash that was a bit like a hardware store being swept away by a thunderstorm. The amazed husband stood waiting for the next storm to break. But it did not break. And he joined the Church the next Sunday. It is evident that our ordinary brand of anger does not look good either in the Bible or out of it.

II

Why is this the case? It is true because so much of our anger is like that of these Pharisees. Why did they get so furious at Jesus on this occasion? What was wrong with their anger?

1. It was purely selfish. They were not interested in this man with his pitiful handicap. They were not concerned with personal values. They were concerned about the law. They felt that a violation of the law governing the Sabbath was an affront to themselves. They felt that the conduct of Jesus tended to weaken their position and to undermine their authority. It therefore wounded their pride. They could endure any amount of injustice toward others, but when their own pet pride was stepped on, it filled them with rage.

Now this is the most common brand of anger among us today. Some of us can stand with complacency any amount of criticism directed against others. It is only when it is directed against ourselves that we become indignant. We can be very sweet-tempered while others are robbed of their rights. It is only when we ourselves are robbed that we get hot and angry. It does not greatly disturb us to see our fellows wounded, but we can let out howls of sheer rage when the wound is suffered by ourselves. About the only time we ever become indignant is when we are not made chairman of the committee, or not invited to the party, or suffer some other affront to our pride.

There was a preacher once that was sent to minister to a great city. He entered that city with a message of doom upon his lips, and with little pity in his heart. He went through its streets shouting, "Yet forty days, and Nineveh shall be destroyed." When the folks heard that startling warning, they were arrested by it. They repented of their sins and thus averted the threatened doom. But Jonah, instead of shouting over it, got angry. "I told these folks," he informed the Lord, all hot and indignant, "that you were going to destroy them, and now you are pardoning them. Such mercy as that will ruin my reputation as a prophet." The sufferings of thousands counted for nothing; his own wounded pride counted for everything. Such anger is utterly hellish.

2. The anger of these Pharisees was not only wrong in its motive, but wrong in its objective. When they got angry, they wanted to destroy the one against whom they were angry. That is what selfish anger always seeks to do. When we are angry at any one, our first impulse is to hurt, to give pain, to wound. Selfish anger is deadly cruel. Sometimes it wounds to the death. How many lives have been snuffed out in a fit of anger! The first impulse of anger is to strike, to become greedy for another's pain.

Now, there are times when our desire for vengeance takes a more refined form. Instead of wounding with our hands, we wound with our tongues. When angry people substitute the sword of their tongues for the sword of steel, they seek to wound; but they strike not at the body, but at the heart. We study to say the thing that we believe will cause the most agony, will bring the deepest shame and humiliation. So eager are we to make the object of our anger writhe that we often have no regard whatever for the truth. We say not only the worst that we know, but what we frankly realize to be false.

Then there are those whose anger takes on a still more refined form. These do not stab either with a dagger or with their tongues. They just break off diplomatic relations. They cease to speak to the object of their anger. They send in their resignation. They quit the game. They withdraw from the Church. They act like the Elder Son in the immortal story that Jesus told. He did not shoot up the town. He just refused to go into the banquet, remained outside and pouted. Why? Because he was trying to hurt somebody. He was eager to cause somebody pain. The some one that he was seeking to hurt was his own kindly father. And his ugly and babyish efforts were not in vain. His father was deeply grieved. Selfish anger, therefore, is always a deadly cruel thing, whether it expresses itself in a fashion that is refined and fastidious, or crass and vulgar.

3. Then this anger of the Pharisees was silly. Our selfish anger always is. We have a way of saying, "I

got mad." It is an altogether proper word. It means that we ceased to act under the impulse of either love or reason. It means that for the time being we became insane. How many foolish and utterly stupid things we say and do when we are angry simply because we have lost our heads!

There was a man in our community when I was a boy who owned and operated a sawmill. He was a good mechanic and had plenty of push and driving power. He should have been a useful and prosperous man. But he had a terrific temper that he did not control. Now and then something would get wrong with his engine. He would set himself to the task of fixing it, but the wrench would slip, or some false move would cause him to hurt himself in some fashion. Immediately there would be an explosion. He would whack the engine with his wrench and then throw the wrench as far as he could into the pond. What was the result? The engine did not burst into tears. It just stopped running. The workers would have to be idle at the expense of the owner while a new piece of machinery was brought from a distant city. At last he went broke, not from lack of ability, but because he could not control his temper. He was too silly to be successful.

But selfish anger is always silly. This is the case not only when we try to wreak our vengeance upon inanimate things; it is even more true when we try to avenge ourselves on others. If I am angry at you, I may wound you, and wound you deeply, but always I will inflict the sorest wound upon myself. When Edmond Dantes escaped from prison, he gave his life to the punishing of those who had wronged him. He made them suffer. But he himself was the greatest sufferer. Selfish anger, therefore, is a deadly and damning thing that we do well to avoid at all cost.

III

But how about the anger of Jesus? His was righteous anger; not because it was his, but it was right in the nature of things.

1. It was right because it was born of a right motive. It was born of love. When Jesus himself was wronged, he bore it. One day a Pharisee invited him to his home. But when Jesus arrived, his host seems to have done his best to make him feel small and uncomfortable. But Jesus was not in the least offended. Later, when his best friend, the man who a few hours before had asserted emphatically that he would go with him to prison and to death, swore that he had never met him, Jesus did not grow indignant. When he turned and looked upon his faltering disciple, there was no anger in his eyes. They were rather full of tenderness and love. Then, at last, when they hung him on the nails and tried to poison the solemn and holy hours of his dying by vile railings, he was not angered in the least. Not once did he try to strike back. It was this, I think, that gripped the heart of Peter as

nothing else. Years later, looking back at those terrible hours, the biggest thing he could say of Jesus was this: "When he was reviled, he reviled not again."

But there were times when Jesus did get angry. When he saw right trodden underfoot of might, then he blazed. When he saw here in the synagogue these religious leaders so totally unmindful of human values, declaring by their conduct that man was made for the Sabbath instead of the Sabbath for man, then he flamed with holy indignation. When on another day he went into the temple and saw how men had made his Father's house into a robbers' cave, that incensed him. When he saw strong men take advantage of the weak, when he saw religious men rob widows' houses and try to atone for it by long prayers, then his eyes flashed fire, and he uttered words that flame to this hour. "Ye serpents," he cries, "ye generation of vipers, how shall you escape the damnation of hell?"

And those who are like Jesus share in his anger. If he were here today, he would burn with holy indignation against all wrong as he did in the long ago. I think his anger would flame against many of us who are trifling with his Church, and thus treating supreme values as if they were worthless gewgaws. He would certainly blaze against those who seek special privileges for themselves and are unmindful of the common good. He would burn with indignation against those men who are willing to make drunkards and orphans and warped and twisted souls for the sake of satisfying their own appetites for drink, or for the sake of growing fat on the proceeds of liquor. He would burn with unspeakable anger, I am sure, against those munition makers who are willing to plunge the whole world into an abysm of blood and tears, if only by so doing they can further smother their souls under an avalanche of profits.

2. It was a righteous anger because it sought a righteous end. When we get angry we wish to hurt. When Jesus got angry it was his passion to help and heal. When he was angry here in the synagogue it was not alone to this man with a handicap that his tender heart went out. It went out no less to these blind and stupid and self-destroyed Pharisees. He rebuked them in "thoughts that breathe and words that burn." But he never hated them; he only hated their sin. Righteous anger is righteous because it seeks to help, and not to hurt.

3. Then the anger of Jesus was sane and dynamic. It was not simply a fit of madness that often leaves its possessor weakened and ashamed. The fire of his anger was what the fire is in a locomotive. It made the steam that gave him driving power. Had he been less passionate he would have accomplished less. It was this holy indignation that helped him to do his work. And what was true of Jesus is true of the greatest of his saints. The outstanding leader of the Old Testament is Moses, and his is the hottest heart in the Old Testament. He could blaze and burn with anger. The greatest man in the New Testament is Paul. And his,

too, is the hottest heart in the New Testament. He could write: "Who is offended, and I do not burn with indignation?"

What, then, shall we do with anger? We shall realize that while selfish anger has no place in the life of a Christian, righteous anger has. The reason most of us blaze so little against the wrongs of our day is not because we are too Christian, but too un-Christian. Much that passes for tolerance among us is not in reality tolerance at all. It is nothing more than indifference. If we loved men as Jesus loved them, we would hate all that oppresses and thwarts them, as he hated it. There is no surer sign that one is rotting down in his inner life than a lost capacity for holy indignation.

Some time ago a young woman told this story. There was a rehearsal for a play. A young bud of a girl who was evidently fresh and clean and modest was openly insulted by the manager. More than a score of men were present when the dirty deed was done. But no cheek glowed in anger, and no eye flashed fire. Why? Because these men were broad and tolerant and Christian? No! It was because their souls had become so honeycombed by moral rottenness that they had lost their capacity for a clean and cleansing anger. Give us men today who can love as Jesus loved, and they will blaze with holy indignation as he blazed. Give us a few such men, and many of the evils that now swagger boldly among us will shrink away in fear, and we will move with irresistible strides toward a better day.

VII

A GLAD SURPRISE

"He was astonished at him."

LUKE 7: 9 (GOODSPEED)

I

HERE IS A MAN WHOSE SERVICE TO THE MASTER was unique. So far as the record goes, he gave Jesus the one glad surprise of his ministry. Our Lord was surprised one other time, but that surprise brought him pain. But this one filled him with boundless joy. You can see the gleam of gladness in his eye and the glow upon his cheek. You can hear the joyous enthusiasm in his voice across the far spaces of the years. There was something in the heart of this Centurion that thrilled him as no miser was ever thrilled by the discovery of hidden gold. What was this priceless treasure? He was amazed by this man's faith. He declared with joyous surprise, "I have not found so great faith, no, not in Israel."

Here, then, in this unsuspected place, Jesus found that treasure upon which he set supreme store. He always gloried in faith. It was the choicest possession of his own soul. Faith was the power by which he lived and did his work. When he hung on the nails the charge that his enemies threw in his face was this, "He trusted in God." Through his own experience he knew that faith was something that made its possessor invincible. He knew that the man of faith can hurl mountains of difficulties into the sea, and break through impossible barriers as though they were a spider's web. No wonder, therefore, he was thrilled by the faith of this Centurion.

II

But why was he so surprised?

1. He was surprised because of who this Centurion was. Such faith in the heart of a Jew would not have been so astonishing. The Jews had as their ancestor a man who was known as the father of the faithful. Their greatest heroes, their greatest prophets and statesmen had been men conspicuous for their faith. They had been trained to faith from their infancy. Jesus expected to find faith among them. The only other time he is represented as being surprised was by their lack of faith. But this Centurion had had no such opportunity. He was a Gentile. He had not been born in a home where one God and one God only was honored. He had grown up under the influence of an enervating polytheism. He had not had a great opportunity. Jesus was astonished, therefore, because he had so little and made so much out of it, just as he

was surprised at the Jews because they had so much and made so little out of it. And if Jesus was astonished at these Jews for their lack of faith, how much greater must be his amazement over us! So many of us believe so little in spite of the fact that our opportunities are far greater than were those of the Jews of Jesus' day.

Not only was this man a Gentile, but he was a Gentile soldier. Now the life of a soldier is not conducive to faith. The profession of killing tends to demoralize and brutalize. This is not to say that there have not been many eminent soldiers who were also eminent Christians. That was far truer of yesterday, I am sure, than it will be of tomorrow. There are many things that our fathers could do and still be saints that we, their sons and daughters, cannot do. New light is constantly breaking upon us, and we must live up to that light or lose our souls.

There was a time, for instance, when one might own slaves and be a Christian, but that would be impossible today. There was a day when even ministers of the gospel might fortify themselves for preaching by taking liquor, but we should not trust such a minister today. One of the sweetest hymns in our hymnal, a song fragrant with the breath of the cross, was written by a man who was engaged in the opium traffic. We are not going to question his Christianity, but we should certainly question the Christianity of such a man today.

And this new day is forcing us to take a new attitude toward war. Amidst our feverish piling up of armaments, there is this encouraging feature: we are facing, as never before, the fact that war is a deadly and damning thing; that it is so deadly and damning as to be the supreme foe of mankind. We have realized that, as horrible as are the brutalities that take place during a wholesale slaughter on the battlefield, this is not the greatest of its evils. The most terrible thing about war is the unmeasured tragedy that follows in its wake. More horrible than the death-dealing shells that we fire when our blood is hot, is the aftermath of broken hopes, blasted ideals, lowered moral standards, wrecked economic systems, blighted bodies, unbalanced minds, and damaged souls. With all these we have to reckon when the smoke of battle is cleared away. Surely it is hard to engage in a business so damning as war and be a man of faith. Yet this Roman soldier had managed it.

2. Not only was Jesus astonished because of who the man was that possessed this faith, he was also astonished at the high quality of his faith. His was a faith strong enough to walk without the crutches of the visible. The Jews needed the assistance of signs. The nobleman whose son Jesus had recently healed is a typical example. "Come down," he prayed. He could not conceive of Jesus' being able to heal at a distance. But this Roman soldier prayed no such prayer. According to Matthew's version, he asked for nothing at all.

He merely laid his desperate plight before the Master, virtually saying to him, "This is my situation; deal with it as you think best." And when Jesus turned his face toward his house he stopped him, saying, "Never mind about coming; just speak the word only, and my slave will get well." How marvelous! No wonder that Jesus was amazed and gladdened. Such a faith creates an atmosphere in which it is possible for him to work. We are not surprised, therefore, that this slave was instantly cured.

III

Now how did this man come by his faith?

This is a vastly important question. It is important because a vital faith is the deepest need of our day. It is the supreme need of the individual. There is nothing that the fathers and mothers who have the shaping of the generation that is to rule the world of tomorrow so need as a genuine faith. It is the supreme need of the Sunday-school teacher. It is the supreme need of every official of the Church. It is the supreme need of the minister. It is the supreme need of the Church as a whole. It is the supreme need of the nation. We can hope for national greatness and national security only through a vital faith in God. How, then, I repeat, did this man find such a faith?

1. His first step was hearing. "Faith cometh by hearing." We must hear before we believe. In the good old days of the mourners' bench, we have heard

some very bewildering instructions given to those who were seeking salvation. "Just believe," some saint would say fervently. "Only believe." But too often this eager teacher would forget to tell the seeker what to believe. "Hold on," another would say. "Just hold on." While yet another would admonish with equal fervor, "Turn loose. Just let go." But unfortunately the inquirer was left in the dark both as to the something that he was to let go, and as to that to which he was to cling. I shall never forget the first man who told me, not simply to believe, but gave me a definite promise on which to rest my faith. Then and there I ventured on that promise and found that it was true.

Now this Roman soldier, coming to live among the Jews, had learned something of their religion. He had been impressed by its high morality. Then, rumors of the teachings and doings of Jesus began to come his way. He was, I imagine, thrilled from the first. "Here is one," he doubtless said, "who seems to embody all that I have dreamed, all that I have longed to be." Then one day he was gripped by a pressing need through the sickness of his slave. While he was struggling under the weight of this burden, I feel confident that this faith was strengthened by the testimony of a friend. That friend was the nobleman whose son Jesus had just healed. These two men lived in the same town, and worked for the same master. This nobleman told him how Jesus, while still at Cana, had cured his boy away at Capernaum. And the Centurion listened and believed.

2. A second step toward victorious faith was obedience. Year by year this Centurion has bravely lived up to the best that he knew. This is ever a sure roadway to faith. There are some for whom faith is far harder than for others. There are those who are beset by intellectual difficulties. There are those who do not believe because of muddy thinking. But there are infinitely more who do not believe because of muddy living. Of all the handicaps to faith, there is none so deadly as disobedience. However clear of vision you may be, if you refuse to be obedient to that vision, it will fade into darkness. However keen of hearing you may be, if you refuse to heed, you will become deaf to the Voice Divine. On the other hand, however dim your vision, if you will live up to it, you will come into the fullness of the light.

(1) He has been loyal to the best that he knows in the use of his money. He has learned that money is power, that this power is not to be used simply for himself, but in the service of others. When these Jewish elders come to plead his cause, they call the Master's attention to the fact that he has built them a synagogue at his own expense. Jesus had doubtless preached in that synagogue. I think it was through its roof that the paralytic was lowered to receive the Master's healing and the Master's forgiveness. Now the man who takes a right relation to his wealth is on the way to a richer

faith. "Prove me now herewith, saith the Lord of hosts, if I will not open you the windows of heaven, and pour you out a blessing, that there shall not be room enough to receive it."

(2) Then this man is beautifully humble. He possesses a winsome modesty that makes him irresistible. When he turns his eyes away from the sufferer in whom he is so keenly interested, and sees Jesus coming to his house, he is overwhelmed by a sense of his own unworthiness. The Master's amazing love fills him with awe. In deep humility he calls some friends who are watching with him and dispatches them posthaste to say to the Master, "Do not trouble yourself further. I am not fit to have you under my roof, nor do I think myself worthy to come to you; but speak the word only, and my servant shall be healed." How beautifully modest! "I am not worthy," he says of himself. But his friends tell a different story. "He is worthy," they say. The man who boasts and swaggers, the man who is constantly praising himself, will usually have a monopoly on that particular job. He will say so much about himself that he will leave nothing to be said by his friends.

This man possesses faith just because he is humble. Pride kills faith. It not only fails to find God, but does not even desire to find Him. Jesus tells the story of two men who one day went to church. It may have been to the same church. One of them was a decent, respectable man. The other man was an outcast, a hireling of a foreign power. They both prayed. But the upright man prayed without humility. He merely thanked God that he was not as other men. The result was that he went down to his house no richer than when he came. Pride had shut the door of blessing in his face. But the publican—he was humble. And through the door of humility he entered into the richness of the forgiving grace of God.

(3) Last of all, and above all, this Roman soldier has lived up to the best that he knows by exercising an unfailing friendliness toward all men. The story of the amazing good will of this man is one of the most winsome that we meet on the pages of the Bible. His friendliness has literally overcome all barriers, and bridged all chasms. First, it has bridged the wide chasm between master and slave. Who is this individual about whom this Roman soldier is so exercised? He is an utter nobody, a slave, a chattel. Yet his master does not look upon him as such. He regards him as a man. He does not even call him slave. He calls him "boy." His friendliness has transformed a slave into a warm, human friend whose sickness breaks his heart, and whose returning health makes him sing.

Then, think how fertile is the soil that his situation offers for the growing of mutual hatred between himself and the people among whom he has come to live. Remember that he is a Roman soldier, a member of a proud and conquering race. Remember, also, that these Jews over whom he has come to stand guard are members of a yet prouder race, in spite of the fact that they have been conquered. All their lives they have been taught to thank God that they were not born Gentiles. Naturally, therefore, they hate their conquerers with a fierce and bitter hatred. Always there are mutterings of rebellion. Again and again this fierce hatred flames into action, to be repressed only by the sternest of measures. Many of their choicest patriots have hung on forests of crosses. And now this Centurion has come to keep up this shameful subjection. No wonder they hate him even before they have ever seen him!

But this soldier meets this hot hate with genuine friendliness. With an invincible good will he bridges the wide chasm of race. He forgets that these among whom he has come to live are turbulent and narrow-minded Jews. He remembers only that they are human beings, men of like passions as himself. Their religion is different from his, but his friendliness bridges that chasm. Then he is the conquerer, and they are the conquered, but his good will even spans that wide chasm. He does not lord it over them. He does not try to make them feel that they are subjects; he ever seeks to make them realize that they are friends. This he does, not for just one day, but for many days. At last he convinces them that he does really care. At last he compels them to this beautiful confession: "He loves us." What an amazing and worth-while victory!

Now, what response do these proud Jews make to this man of good will? Well, they simply find it impossible to continue to hate him. In fact, they find it impossible to refrain from loving in return. When, therefore, trouble comes to his home and he is anxious and worried, they do not rejoice over it. They do not declare that God is punishing him for his sins. Instead, they gather about him, eagerly asking if there is anything they can do. When he tells them that they might see Jesus on his behalf, they are all eagerness. They hurry away and present his plea as forcefully and earnestly as possible.

It worked then. It will work today. A friend of mine tells this story. A certain friend of his, who was an unusually beautiful Christian, bought a lovely home in the suburbs of one of our Southern cities. He had his goods moved out one day, but he himself did not arrive till the late afternoon. While he was out walking over the wide lawn that was part of his newly acquired property, he saw his next-door neighbor hurrying to meet him. He was glad, for he was always eager to make friends. But this neighbor did not greet him in the kindly fashion that he had expected. "Did you buy this property?" he asked in a voice tense with anger. "Yes," came the quiet reply. "Well, you have bought a lawsuit, that's all. That fence is seven feet over on my land, and I am going to have every inch of what is mine if it costs me the last dollar I have."

Now, what answer would you have made to an onslaught like that? I tell you what this Christian did. He said, "My friend, there is no need of a lawsuit. I believe that you are perfectly sincere in what you say. Therefore, though I bought this land in good faith, I am not going to claim it. I will have that fence moved the first thing in the morning." The angry man looked at his new neighbor in wide-eyed amazement. "What did you say? Do you really mean that you will have this fence moved?" "That is exactly what I mean," came the quiet answer. Then the astonished neighbor broke into a string of oaths that were about as earnest as prayers. "Blankety, blank, blank," he said, "no, you won't. This fence is going to stay right where it is. Any man that is as white as you are can have the blank land. And that's not all, you can have anything else that I have that you want." Thus he won his neighbor by his invincible good will.

Are you desirous of a larger faith? Do you yearn for a faith that will satisfy your own deep needs and make you a transmitter of the power of God to a needy world? You can have it. This is just as certain as that you are listening to me at this moment. It is as sure as the fact of God. You will find it if you walk the road that this man walked—the road of obedience. Begin here and now to use your money as God's steward, to walk in humility, to meet the world with an invincible good will, and then one day you, too, will come to a radiant faith that will be a surprise to your own heart. You, too, will thrill your Lord with unspeakable joy as did this Centurion of the long ago.

Stilling the Sea

VIII

DEFEATING OUR FEARS

"... *Why are you afraid?*"

MATTHEW 8: 26 (MOFFATT)

JESUS WITH HIS DISCIPLES IS CROSSING THE SEA of Galilee. He is a bit weary, therefore he goes into the stern of the boat, makes himself as comfortable as possible upon a pillow, and is soon fast asleep. While he is sleeping, a sudden storm breaks upon them. The savage winds soon lash the sea into wild fury. The waves begin to spit their rage into the face of heaven, and to toss the puny vessel as a juggler might toss a ball. At first the disciples bear up bravely. Some of them are men of the sea and are not easily frightened. They will hold on their course in spite of the storm. But their situation becomes more threatening each moment. Meantime, they begin to turn perplexed and fear-filled faces toward their Master. Is he never going to awake? Is it possible that with Death blowing its chilling breath in their very faces he is going to sleep through it all?

At last they can stand the strain no longer. They are loath to wake him, but they feel that they must. Therefore, frantic with fear, one grasps him rudely by the shoulder and shakes him into wakefulness. "Master, wake up," he cries; "don't you care if we drown?" It is a very human question. It has been asked in one way or another countless millions of times. Jesus opens his eyes, rebukes the sea, and there is a great calm. Then he turns to these friends of his and asks in bewilderment not unmixed with pain, "Why are you afraid?" And strange to say, these men who could have given such an excellent reason for their fears a few moments ago are utterly silent now. Their terrors seem positively silly in the presence of this Man who speaks to them with such calm confidence, and looks at them with such quiet eyes.

"Why are you afraid?" This is a question that Jesus is constantly asking. He asked it long ago when life was haunted by so many fears. He is asking it in the enlightened day in which we live.

1. This is the case because fear is so widespread. So many of us are afraid. Poor folks are afraid. Of course. They have no sense of economic security. They do not know how they are going to keep the "wolf of want" from their doors. But many rich, who are fairly smothered in their luxuries, are even more afraid. The ignorant and superstitious are frightened. They do not know when a black cat might run across their pathways or they might get a glimpse of the new moon in an unlucky fashion. But many who are educated are also constantly dogged by fears. Irreligious

people—those who have no sense of God in their lives —have fears. But sad to say, this is also true of many who belong to the Church and who are earnestly religious. Old folks who are coming close to the sunset and evening star are sometimes fearful. Their strength is failing and they know that their day will soon be over. But many who are in life's green spring are even more afraid. Fear constantly dogs the steps of vast multitudes in every walk of life.

Then we are afraid of all sorts of things. We fear for the health of our bodies and for the health of our souls. We are afraid that we cannot secure a desirable position, or that we may lose the one that we have. We are afraid of what happened yesterday, it may track us down and bring us shame. We are afraid of what might happen tomorrow. Tomorrow some lurking tragedy may spring upon us and lay waste our lives. We are afraid for ourselves. We are afraid for our children. We are afraid for our friends. We are afraid lest someone may get ahead of us. We are afraid of what others may think or say about us. We begin, psychologists tell us, with only two fears, but soon they become a multitude. There is nothing too big or too insignificant to make us afraid.

2. Then this question is pertinent because fear is so harmful. There are few foes so utterly ruinous as fear. This is true in spite of the fact that fear has a legitimate place in our lives. There are fears that safeguard and protect us. The man, therefore, who

tells us that he is absolutely afraid of nothing is not speaking complimentarily of himself. There are certain things of which every sane man ought to be afraid. For instance, every man ought to be afraid to take a needless physical risk. Life is far too priceless to be flung away for naked nothing. There are many high values for which we may wisely venture our all, but to venture that all for nothing is plain stupidity. The man, for example, who is not afraid to mix gasoline and liquor is not showing himself to be wise, but foolish. We ought to be afraid of needlessly violating the laws of health. Every sane man ought to be afraid to take any needless physical risk.

Then every sane man ought to be afraid to take a needless moral risk. Everyone, therefore, who flirts with uncleanliness and everyone who toys with some practice that is likely to enslave him is simply playing the fool. This was the trouble with Samson. He thought he was smart enough to have his fling and get away with it. He therefore exposed himself to the direst moral risks. But regardless of the fact that he was not afraid, his venture cost him his freedom and ultimately his life. The man who is not afraid of sin does not for that reason escape fear. He only makes his bondage to fear an absolute certainty. For every man who is not afraid of sin sooner or later is made afraid by his sin. In the old Genesis story, the first face upon which Adam looked after he broke with God was the face of Fear. Every wise man, therefore, will be afraid of a needless moral risk.

But it is not of our legitimate fears that I propose to speak now. I am to speak rather of our foolish and needless fears. It is these that do so much to mar and lay waste our lives.

II

What do these fears do to us? Why are they so ruinous?

1. Fear is creative: "The thing which I greatly feared is come upon me." This pathetic wail that we hear from the lips of Job is the soundest psychology. The experience of this ancient sufferer has been that of countless multitudes. Fear is always creating the thing it dreads. The man who is constantly fearing for his health—the one who gets up every morning with his fingers upon his pulse and with his tongue poked out before the mirror—that is the man who is most likely to be sick. I have a friend who rushes home and makes his will every time he hears of any sort of epidemic, even one so common as colds. He constantly goes about armed with various remedies. He haunts the offices of doctors. He is therefore sick, or fancies himself so, about 365 days each year. Fear tends to create the thing it fears.

Then fear is creative in another sense. It is creative in that it is contagious. When I was a country schoolteacher, I remember a story—a fairly silly story

—that was in one of our readers. It told how Chicken Little was in the garden one morning when a cabbage leaf fell upon her tail. She at once concluded that the sky was falling. Therefore, crazed with terror, she began to run. By and by, she met Henny Penny and told her the fearful story. Seized by panic, she, too, began to run. Soon all the other fowls of the barnyard heard the horrible news and joined in the stampede. Off they went, running for their lives. At last, they met Mr. Fox, who offered them refuge in his den, where he made of them a gorgeous feast. Now, we men and women are very much like that, and can be stampeded almost as easily. By our fears, we can take the heart out of others. Fear is contagious.

2. Fear makes us wretched. If we are to find life joyous, we must get rid of fear. What agony, born of sheer fear, have we seen in the faces of men and women. At its mildest, fear is a kill-joy. At its worst, it is very hell. A few years ago I read the story of a hobo who slipped into an empty banana car to steal a ride to a neighboring city. He lay down upon a pile of straw and soon dropped off to sleep. By and by, he was awakened by something crawling on his face and hands. He brushed it away, but the crawling kept on. At last he sprang to his feet, more annoyed than afraid. He fumbled in his pockets for a match, and found only one. This he struck and held aloft till it burned his fingers. He was too frightened to be at once conscious of the pain, for the straw seemed alive with tarantulas. When

the match had gone out and black darkness had fallen upon him, he sprang for the door only to find it fast. He then proceeded to pound it till his fists were bloody. But there was no response. When he was released the next morning, he was little better than a maniac. This was the case not because of any physical pain. Not a single tarantula had harmed him. He was driven half mad by fear. Fear is a sure road to wretchedness.

3. Then fear is paralyzing. When I was a student at Harvard University, for quite a season, I used to meet each morning, as I went to my first class, a huge dog. Now I am afraid of dogs. I do not need any psychiatrist to tell me why. I was bitten by one when I was a child. But I spoke to this dog at each meeting as if I loved him. But he seemed to sense my lack of sincerity, and to resent it. At least, when we met one day he made no polite response to my greeting. Instead, when he was a few feet past me, he wheeled with a roar and came at me. And I did just what all dog psychologists say do. I stood perfectly still and looked him squarely in the eye. But this I did, not because I knew it was the wisest course—I did it because I was scared stiff.

What was the matter with the man of one talent? It was not that circumstances were against him. It was not that a man with such a meager gift has no chance —he had every chance. He was afraid. Therefore, he did nothing but bury his talent in the earth. Why did not the Rich Young Ruler follow Jesus? It was not because Jesus did not appeal to him. He did appeal and that greatly. This young ruler was paralyzed by fear. Why do we so often do nothing in the presence of appalling wrongs? We are afraid. Too often we are so afraid that we will do the wrong thing, that we do nothing at all.

4. Not only does fear tend to paralyze, thus preventing our doing what we know we ought to do, it often drives us to do things that we know we ought not to do. How many lies we tell, not because we are naturally dishonest, but because we are afraid. Why do such a vast number of women smoke cigarettes today? It is not because they have any greater desire for tobacco than their sisters of a few years ago. Smoking became a fad, and they were afraid not to conform. Why do so many, who have been reared in homes where liquor was never allowed, join in the drinking of cocktails today? It is not the result, at least at the beginning, of any appetite for liquor. They drink because they are afraid to say "No." Fear often leads us to spit in the face of our deepest convictions. "The fear of man," says the wise man, "bringeth a snare." That has been proved true countless millions of times.

Not only does fear often cause us to outrage our convictions by engaging in practices to which we object, it often makes us cruel. This is true of the group. Fear is perhaps the supreme factor in bringing about the red hell of war. It is true also of the individual. Some time ago, I read anew the story of the sinking of the Titanic. The writer said that many of the lifeboats that put out from this ill-fated vessel were not half full. Yet people by the hundreds were left behind to drown. Why this cruelty? It was born of fear. The author told of a certain swimmer who succeeded in making his way to one of these half-empty boats. He clutched the side and tried to climb in. But no one lent him a hand. Not only so, but a woman took an oar and pounded his hands until he could cling no longer, and he dropped back to his death. Why did she do that? It was not because there was no room in the boat, there was plenty. She was brutalized by fear. Fear at its worst blasts our convictions and changes us into beasts.

III

If fear then is such a ruinous and deadly thing, we ought to be rid of it—but how?

Well, we cannot be rid of it by simply clinching our fists and resolving to banish it altogether. There are certain fears that might be banished in some measure by this method, but this is not enough. In one of McGuffey's readers, there is a story of a lad who saw a guidepost one night, and was terrified by it. In the gloom it looked like a forbidding monster. But when he discovered what it really was, he was ashamed of his foolish fears. He then reached the following conclusion:

"Ah well," thought he, "one thing I've learned,
Nor shall I soon forget;
Whatever frightens me again
I'll march right up to it!"

That might serve for the specters of the mind. But it would be a poor way out if what you feared happened to be a rattlesnake or a speeding car. Our cure must go deeper than this.

Nor are we going to get rid of our fears by simply ignoring them. There are some foes that we fear that are very real. Since they are so, we are not going to destroy our fear of them by merely shutting our eyes. There are those, for instance, who seek thus to banish sin, sickness, and death. But these grim realities persist, however hard we try to ignore them. Since we know this, our fears are likely to persist, unless we find a better remedy. Too often, when we say we are not afraid of these things, we simply drive our fear down into the subconscious mind and thus sow the seed for future trouble.

How then can we conquer fear? One prime essential, as others have pointed out, is the living of a clean and upright life. No man can be really fearless who hides guilty secrets in his heart. If your yesterday has been stained by faithlessness or crime, the nemesis of fear is upon your track today. Think of the tormenting fears of Arthur Dimmesdale in Hawthorne's *Scarlet Letter*. Nobody knew his guilt save himself and the woman who shared his sin. But every moment of his waking existence was a hellish nightmare of fear. Think of the terror that dogs the steps of the professional criminal. Many a fugitive from justice has surrendered of his own accord, because he felt that the penitentiary, or even the gallows, would be better than being tortured by the fiendish fears that constantly hung upon his heels. To be rid of fear then, a clean and upright life is an absolute necessity.

But the supreme antidote against fear is faith. "Why are you afraid?" Jesus asks; and then he adds this further word, "How little you trust God." By this he means to say that fear and faith cannot at the same time keep house in the same heart. When faith comes in, fear flees like a guilty thing afraid. Jesus knew this from his own experience. His was a tempestuous life. When he began his ministry, there was a bit of calm, but soon the skies were overcast. He had to see his popularity change into hate. He had to face day by day the bitterest of opposition. At last, he had to see the high mission to which he had given his life seemingly fall into utter ruins. He himself was nailed to the cross. But through it all, there was never a moment of fear. In the face of defeat and death, he bore himself with a calm courage at which all the centuries have wondered. What was his secret? It is found in the words that were howled at him by the mob that watched him die. "He trusted in God." A faith like that of Jesus makes fear an utter impossibility.

Now this faith that casts out fear is a big and brawny

something. It is far more than a mere belief that we have a good and fatherly God who will keep us out of all difficulties. A faith that expects God to still all storms may calm our fears for a while, but such relief is only temporary. We shall become only the more fearful when we realize that God does not save us from all hard situations. When these disciples appealed to Jesus, he stilled the storm, but others who have prayed just as earnestly have gone down at sea. "God sends his rain upon the just and the unjust." The same also is true of droughts. In the old Sunday-school stories, there were usually a good boy and a bad boy. The good boy was always coming out on top and the bad boy was forever getting stung. But that is not altogether true to life. Bad men do sometimes go to the wall, but so do good men. A man's faithlessness often gets him into trouble, but so does his faithfulness. It was Paul's faithfulness that caused him to be scarred from head to foot by the stones and scourges of persecution. A faith, therefore, that saves from fear must be more than a faith that expects deliverance from hardship and difficulty.

What then is this faith? It is a faith that trusts God so completely that it puts His will first in all things. It is a faith that believes that the will of God is so perfect that nothing can harm us so long as we live within that will. This was the faith that gave Paul his undaunted courage. "We know," he declares boldly, "that to them that love God, all things work together for good." If a man is really convinced of that in the deepest depths of his soul, then nothing can make him afraid. He may be called upon to face loneliness, unpopularity, bitter loss, intense suffering. But these will not frighten him because he knows that God can change his foes into friends, his calamities into capital, his losses into gains. "This is the victory that overcometh the world" with all of its fears and with all of its terrors—"even our faith." If we trust God enough to put His will first, if we have no fear save the fear of disappointing Him, then that fear will banish all others as the sunrise banishes the stars.

Casting Out Demons

IX

THE DISTURBING CHRIST

"And they began to pray him to depart out of their coasts."

MARK 5: 17

I

HAD YOU PASSED THROUGH THIS VILLAGE OF Gerasa a week before the events here recorded, you would doubtless have been impressed by its quiet restfulness. There was an atmosphere of contentment that pervaded the people, as

"Along the cool sequestered vale of life
They kept the noiseless tenor of their way."

Even that notorious madman, who now and then stirred a few waves of excitement upon the sea of their complacency, was behaving fairly well. At least, he was living among the tombs down by the lake. Perhaps, not recently, had he upset the villagers by coming to town and getting himself bound with fetters and with chains.

But today, all this is changed. The once placid calm

has given place to a fever of excitement. If you have ever gone into the forest in early spring and overturned a rotting log and watched the twilight life that had its home underneath as it scurried here and there; if you have heard, even with the ears of your imagination, these disturbed creatures shriek at you to go away and stop annoying them, you can appreciate what is happening among these villagers. They are being disturbed by the new light that is shining upon them. They do not like it. Therefore, their one prayer is to be let alone.

Who has caused this fever of excitement? Who has dared to shake them, for the moment at least, out of the deep ruts in which they were so content to abide? It is none other than the Young Carpenter from Nazareth. He is doing here what he was constantly doing throughout his entire ministry. He is doing here what he has done through all the subsequent centuries. He is the most disturbing personality that the world has ever known. I know that he comes to us with the promise of rest. But he usually has to make us restless before he can give us rest. He is a persistent disturber.

One Sabbath day, for instance, he attended services at his own home church. He stood up to signify that he desired to read the lesson for the day. He turned to that thrilling passage in Isaiah that begins, "The Spirit of the Lord is upon me." Having read, he began to tell them how that scripture was then and there being fulfilled. At first, the people listened, charmed by his gracious words. But he proceeded to tell them that, while they might be God's children, they were not his only children. This was indicated by the fact that while there were many widows in Israel during the days of Elijah, when God wanted somebody to provide for his prophet, he sent him, not to one of themselves, but to a woman who was a pagan. He told them that, while there were many lepers in Israel during the days of Elisha, not a single one of them had the faith to be cured. The only one that was healed was a man without the covenant, named Naaman. And the service that had begun so peacefully broke up in a riot.

When Jesus was brought before Pilate, most of the testimony given against him was utterly false. But there was one bit that was true. His enemies declared that he had stirred up the people throughout the whole nation. There was no denying that. He did throw the people of his day into a ferment of excitement. And he has been disturbing us ever since—this strange Man upon his cross. Since then, he has lifted empires off their hinges and changed the whole course of human history. Jesus was and is the supreme disturber.

II

How does Jesus disturb us?

1. Our Lord disturbs us by the very processes of living in the kind of world in which he has placed us. Ours is a world of constant flux and change. Nothing

remains quite the same. No sooner do we adopt one style of dress than we have to throw it away for another. No sooner do we accept one mode of travel than we have to discard it for another. We changed our oxcarts and prairie schooners for horses and buggies. We changed our horses and buggies for automobiles and airships. We throw away our candles for kerosene lamps, and these we must exchange for the incandescent. We discard our old books for new ones. We exchange the statement of the faith of our fathers for one more suited to our own needs. We leave the old home to establish one of our own, only to have this one broken up, in its turn, by the ruthless hand of change. To live in a world like ours is constantly to be disturbed.

This is the case whether we like it or not. A great many of us do not like it. We do not accept change graciously. We like to sink down complacently into our well-worn ruts and be at ease. But life refuses to treat us that way. The passing years bring changes that all but compel us to make new adventures. To refuse to do so, is to be thrown into discard. You remember that lovely old couple in Goethe's *Faust,* who stood in the way of the building of the City Beautiful. They refused to accept change, so one night their house burned to the ground and they burned with it. Our Lord is constantly saying to us what he said to the children of Israel long ago, "You have dwelt long enough in this mountain." Day by day we are being called to strike our tents and move on to other camping grounds. We are born on an incline—everyone of us—where there is no standing still. We must either climb or slip down the hill. Our Lord is constantly disturbing us by setting us to live in a changing world.

2. He disturbs us by being what He is. In his presence, we see ourselves. One day, a city missionary sat by the bedside of an outcast woman who was ill. She was not talking to this woman about her sins, she was simply paying her a friendly visit. But suddenly, the sick woman burst into tears. As her visitor sought the reason, this woman of the street reached out her thin finger and touched the white flower that her friend held in her hand. "I am not like that," she said; "I used to be white like that, but I am not any more." Against the white background of that lovely flower, this woman had seen herself.

It is in some such fashion that Jesus disturbs us. Our first impression as we come into his presence is this, "I am not like that." We can compare ourselves with each other with fair complacency. "I am not anything to brag on," a chap said the other day, "but I am as good as the average." Possibly so, but we do not talk like that in the presence of Jesus. When we see ourselves against the white background of his pure and radiant life, we cry with Isaiah, "Unclean, unclean."

Here, for instance, is a robber who is dying by the most fiendish mode of torture that the ingenuity of man has ever contrived. This man has led a hard and bloody life. He has been a highwayman, a knight of the road.

He has swooped down upon his fellows as ruthlessly as a beast of prey. But now he has reached the end of the trail. He is suffering the pangs of death. But, as he thus suffers, he declares that it is just, that he is receiving the due rewards of his deeds. How has he come to make such a confession? None such is being made by his fellow in crime. What has happened? This man has seen himself and his deeds against the white background of the personality of Jesus. Therefore, as he suffers the very pangs of hell, he cries, "I suffer justly." As we see Jesus, we see ourselves.

Not only does Jesus disturb us by showing us ourselves, he disturbs us no less by showing us what we may become. If, when we stand in his presence, our first word is, "I am not like that," our second surely is this: "I may be like that. As he used his life, so I ought to use mine. As he flung himself away for the good of others, so ought I to fling myself away. I am not like him, but I can be, I ought to be, I long to be like him." So men felt who really saw him in the long ago. So they feel to this day. Jesus is constantly disturbing us by compelling us to see the larger and better men and women that he makes it possible for us to be.

3. Then our Lord disturbs us by the call of human need. Here is a story from the life of St. Paul. He is telling us how he came to invade Europe with his revolutionary gospel. One night in Troas, he had a vision

of a man of Macedonia. The hungry face of this man so haunted him as to make restful indifference impossible. His outstretched hands were so appealing as to disturb his very dreams. To his ears there came a call as disquieting as the call of a sick and frightened child to its mother. "Come over into Macedonia and help us," was the appeal. That appeal made further sleep for Paul impossible. It upset his plans. It compelled him to new adventures. Our Lord was disturbing him by the call of human need.

So men have been disturbed through all the centuries. They have been made restless and eager by the needs, the burdens, heart-hungers of their fellows. "Why do you wish to return to China?" Dr. Jowett asked of a missionary who had come home as an invalid. "Because I cannot sleep at night for thinking of them," came the answer. The empty lives of those who needed him took the softness out of his bed and stuffed his pillow with thorns. Why did Walter Reed and his companions brazenly flirt with death in their fight with yellow fever? They had been disturbed by the call of human need. Thus through the years, our Lord has disturbed heroic men and women who have gone forth to brave all sacrifices and to dare all deaths in order to serve their fellows. These have been so disquieted by their brothers' burdens that they could find no peace till they took them upon themselves.

And our amazing Christ is doing today what he has always done. He is disturbing some of us by the needless suffering and the needless waste of life among underprivileged people of other lands, and we are going as missionaries. He is disturbing others by the injustices of our own social order so that they must be giving themselves to the changing of the things that are into the things that ought to be. Our fathers looked upon war with more or less complacency. But this is today impossible for an ever-increasing multitude. We are being disturbed by it. We are realizing that war really is hell, and that we must learn to live together or we are not going to live at all. Our Lord is calling us through this great need to give ourselves to the high task of peace-making. Thus, through what he is, through the very process of living, through the call of need, through countless other voices, our Lord is disturbing us.

III

Why does Jesus disturb us?

He does not disturb us because he enjoys our restlessness. It seems hard for some of us to get away from that strange conviction that religion is a kill-joy. "Pale Galilean, Thou hast conquered, and the world has grown gray at Thy birth." But really a more colossal lie was never told. About all the radiance and beauty that has come to our world has come through this amazing birth. But in spite of this fact, there are still those who seem to feel that Jesus has come "to steal and to kill and to destroy," rather than to give us life in abundance. You remember how Thomas Hardy ends one of his depressing stories. Tess has died after meaningless suffering. "Thus," concludes the author, "the President of the Immortals had finished his sport with Tess." His idea seems to be that the God whom Jesus came to reveal is, after all, only a cruel devil who takes pleasure in torturing His own children.

Now, our Lord does disturb us. He frankly tells us that he has come not to send peace, but a sword. But this does not mean that he does not give peace to those who give him a chance. He is the Prince of peace. Giving peace is his specialty. "Peace I leave with you, my peace I give unto you." What, then, does he mean? He means that he has not come to bring a wrong kind of peace. There is a peace that is born of stagnation and death. He must often take his sharp sword and stab us into wakefulness and restlessness before he can give us real peace. But he never disturbs us just because he delights in our unhappiness. He does not disturb us because being disturbed is an end in itself.

Why then, I repeat, does he disturb us? He does so in order to bring us to the realization of our best possibilities. Not to be disturbed is to sink into a complacent self-content. To be content with ourselves, to be content with things as they are, means arrested development. Such contentment strikes a deathblow to all progress either for the individual or for the group. If we are as good as we desire to be, we are not likely to become any better. If we are as wise as we care to be, we are not going to grow any wiser. If we are as high up the hill as we long to be, we are not going to climb any higher. It is only as our Lord disturbs us that he can get us to move on.

In one of the most tenderly beautiful and poetic passages in the Old Testament, God's care of His people is compared to that of the mother eagle for her young. "For the Lord's portion is his people; Jacob is the lot of his inheritance. He found him in a desert land, and in the waste howling wilderness; he led him about, he instructed him, he kept him as the apple of his eye. As an eagle stirreth up her nest, fluttereth over her young, spreadeth abroad her wings, taketh them, beareth them on her wings: so the Lord alone did lead him, and there was no strange god with him." That is, God disturbs us as the mother eagle disturbs her young when she stirreth her nest. There are the eaglets safe and comfortable in their rugged home high upon a shelf of the cliffs. But one day, the mother comes without bringing her young their accustomed food. Instead of feeding them, with ruthless claws, she tears their home into shreds. Not only so, but she flings them from their place of safety out into space. Helpless and frightened, they begin to fall to where the ragged rocks are waiting to pound out their lives.

Why does this mother do this seemingly cruel thing? Is it that she may laugh in fiendish glee at the terror of her falling young? Not a bit of it. She does not allow them to fall. Just when they are thinking that they are doomed, she dashes underneath them, takes them upon her wings and bears them up so that they suffer no hurt. What, then, is she trying to do? She is trying to teach these eaglets to realize that for which they were born. They were not made simply to be coddled in safety. They were made for the cloudland and for the upper air. They were not made to be sheltered in a nest. They were made "to bathe their plumage in the thunder's home." And that is the reason that our Lord disturbs us. We, too, are meant for flight sunward and Godward. As our Master, we have not come to be ministered unto, but to minister. Therefore, our Lord is constantly seeking to arouse us from a low content in order to bring us to our best.

IV

Now, what response are we to make to this disturbing Christ? When our Lord awakens us, what are we to do about it? This is the big question. It is not ours to decide whether we shall or shall not be disturbed. Again and again our Lord awakens us, whether we will it or not. Again and again his voice breaks upon our indifference and complacency, even though we may be unwilling. But, while it is not ours to decide whether we shall be disturbed or not, it is ours to decide what we shall do, once we are disturbed. If an alarm clock rings in your room, it is likely to wake you whether you wish it to or not. But when it has gotten you awake, that is as far as it can go. It cannot drag you out of bed. Whether you get up or go back to sleep depends entirely upon yourself. And that, with all reverence, is as far as our Lord can go. All he can do is to disturb us. This he does in a thousand ways. But having done that, the rest is left to us. He can wake us, but the getting up must be done by ourselves.

Now, what response do we make? Broadly speaking, we make one of two. We either get up or we remain in bed and go back to sleep. These villagers took the latter course. They were disturbed by Jesus, but nothing worthwhile came of it. All the change it made in their lives was to cause them to hurry to him with this terrible prayer upon their lips, "Depart out of our coasts." He was interfering with their business. They were afraid that he would cut down their profits. Therefore, there was but one thing for them to do and that was to get rid of him.

You will agree that theirs is a terrible prayer. Yet awful as it is, there is not one of us that has not at some time prayed it. Of course, we do not word it just as they did. We never quite dare to say to Jesus openly and frankly, "Leave us alone." But we tell him to do so in language just as emphatic. This we do by refusing to give up some practice to which we know he objects. This we do when we are content with the second best, when he is calling us to the best. We thus pray when we turn a deaf ear to needs that we know we ought to meet, when we stand idle in the presence of pressing calls to which we know we ought to respond.

We have all, at one time or another, asked to be let alone. Some of us are praying that prayer even now.

What response does Jesus make to such terrible prayers? He makes the only one that he can make. He grants our request. So he did in the case of these Gerasenes. So he ever does. When he stopped on one occasion to spend the night in a certain Samaritan village, they refused to receive him. What then? He did not call down fire from heaven as the Sons of Thunder asked him to do. He did something more tragic still. He passed on to the next village. Our Lord will not and cannot force himself upon any of us. Persistently, he stands at the door and knocks. But it is ours to open. If we fail, we little by little get used to being without him, till we all but cease to care. There is more of truth and pathos even than of humor and poetry in those words of Kenneth C. Kaufman:

> "I think my soul is a tame old duck,
> Dabbling around in barnyard muck,
> Fat and lazy, with useless wings.
> But sometimes when the north wind sings,
> And the wild ones hurtle overhead,
> It remembers something lost and dead,
> And cocks a wary and bewildered eye,
> And makes a feeble attempt to fly.
> It's fairly content with the state it's in,
> But it isn't the duck it might have been." [1]

But if it is within our power to resist our Lord when

[1] From *Level Land*, published by Kaleidograph Press, Dallas. Originally published in the *Daily Oklahoman*. Used by permission.

he disturbs us, it is also within our power to yield to him. If we can say "No" to him, we can also say "Yes." And it is this that makes the real difference between the spiritually victorious and those who go down in defeat—one yields to God's awakenings, the other does not. How great was the disturbance that our Lord wrought in the heart of Paul! After he had witnessed the stoning of Stephen, he was a haunted man. His soul was as a sea whipped by a tempest. He could never forget the shining face and the Christlike prayer of that great saint. But the disturbance wrought in the heart of Paul was no more real than that wrought in the soul of profligate Felix under Paul's preaching. As the great apostle reasoned of righteousness, temperance, and judgment, he was made to shudder. But here the similarity ends. Felix said, "Go thy way for this time," and sank into the sleep of death. Paul said, "Lord, what wilt thou have me do?" and henceforth went to live in the freshness and beauty of an eternal springtime. Which course will you take?

Healing the Demoniac

X
GREAT THINGS

"Go home to thy friends, and tell them how great things the Lord hath done for thee."

MARK 5: 19

THE STORY OF WHICH THIS TEXT IS A PART HAS certain details that are thoroughly bewildering. Some of its language sounds like a foreign tongue to our modern ears. But we must not allow this fact to blind us to its central message. This queerness as to details has to do with the nonessentials of the story, rather than with its essential truth. It has to do with the setting of the jewel, rather than the jewel itself. And there is real jewelry here and that of priceless worth. This story tells what Christ did for a poor demented wreck in the long ago. It tells also what he does today for the soul that gives him a chance.

He does "great things!" I like that word. There are many who seem to think that our religion has in it more of weight than of wings; that at best, its benefits are rather paltry and worthless trifles. But in reality, these seeming trifles are the great things, the priceless things, the supreme things. "Tell how great things the Lord hath done for thee." Have you such a story to tell? Is there anything taking place in your life day by day that can only be described by this word "great"? If there is nothing, then you are not claiming your spiritual birthright. If there is nothing, then your religion is not doing for you what God intended that it should do. But this is not the fault of your Lord, nor is it the fault of the Church. It is your own fault. Wherever Christ has his way, he does great things. Such was the case here. Such has been the case throughout the centuries.

I

Look at this man as Jesus found him. The description given of him is so clear that it would seem to have come from the pen of an eyewitness. The keel of the boat in which Jesus is sailing has hardly touched the shore before a ghastly figure rushes out from one of the tombs. He is wearing practically no clothing. He is disheveled and unkempt. To his wrists and ankles probably still cling the fragments of fetters with which men have vainly tried to bind him. He is a poor half-mad creature with whom we feel little kinship. But when we face the facts, we are made to realize that we have much in common. Of course, we are far more sane than he, far more decent and respectable. Yet we differ from him in degree rather than in kind. This we realize as we study his story. What was the matter with him?

1. He was a divided personality. When Jesus asked him his name, he gave a ready answer: "My name is Legion." That is, he was not one, but many. He was not so much a personality, as H. G. Wells would say, as a battleground. He was at war with himself. He was being tugged in a thousand different directions. A thousand different impulses and passions were warring within his soul. We meet such divided and disintegrating personalities today in the psychopathic wards of our hospitals. But we do not find them there alone. We often meet them as we mingle with our fellows. We sometimes even meet such as we live with ourselves. Of course, this inner conflict is far less pronounced with some than with others. But all of us know something of the tragedy of a divided personality.

The truth of this is emphasized by modern psychologists. They tell us, for instance, that we are possessed of a conscious and a subconscious mind. In the subconscious mind are the driving instincts that have come to us from our ancestors. These instincts are without conscience. They have no moral sense. They seek their gratification, the pleasure of their own fulfillment, with not the slightest attention to the question of right and wrong. But in the conscious mind, there is a sense of oughtness. Here is that which makes us say "I owe" and "I must," or "I must not." Therefore, the conscious mind rises up against the subconscious. Our ideals fight with our instincts. Our higher self battles with our lower self. Hence we become divided personalities, incarnate civil wars, victims of the direst of all conflicts—the conflict within ourselves.

The writers of the Bible discovered this long before the birth of modern psychology. Here is a man, for instance, who is conscious within himself that he fears the Lord. He is a man of piety and prayer. Even now, he is upon his knees with his face turned wistfully toward the heights. But there is another self within him that refuses to kneel. There is another self that jeers and sneers while the higher self seeks to pray. It is out of the agony of this conflict that he cries to God. For what does this earnest soul make request? What is his prayer? This: "Unite my heart to fear Thy name." He has a fear of the Lord that is altogether genuine. But in spite of this, he is conscious that he is only half-hearted in his fear. He is, therefore, praying for a unified personality, a wholehearted devotion to God.

Here is another man who is also deeply religious. But he seems more sensitive to the lure of evil than to that of good. He is more conscious of the call of the depths than the call of the heights. He has a keener sense of his baser self than he has of his better self. The voices that call to him to take the lower road seem more appealing than those that call to him to take the higher. But in spite of this, he cannot wholly give himself to the base and to the unclean. He cannot fling himself with abandon away from all that is beautiful and best. He has gone into the far country of his own choice, yet he cannot be at home there. Therefore, he cries, "My soul cleaveth unto the dust: quicken thou me according to thy word." If with one hand he is grasping at the mud, with the other he is reaching for the stars. Therefore, like this demoniac and like ourselves, he is at war with himself.

2. This poor fellow, being at war with himself, was naturally wretched. "Always, night and day," the story says, "he was crying and cutting himself with stones." Always he was fighting himself. Always he was wounding himself. Always he was his own worst enemy. Thus warring against himself, he was a stranger to real happiness. That is ever the case. No divided personality can ever be happy. However beautiful our surroundings, however large our bank account, however great our success, however thunderous the applause that may ring in our ears—if we are at war with ourselves, we are miserable and will continue to be so till our conflict is hushed into peace.

This is not theory, this is experience. Here is a great soul that is in the midst of this age-old conflict. He is lured by the heights. But when he sets out to climb, he somehow gravitates toward the depths. He hates the unclean and solemnly vows that he will never stretch forth his hand to it again. But while his vow is yet upon his lips, he finds himself guilty of the very deed that he has solemnly foresworn. At last in desperation he utters a wild cry that comes to us across the far spaces of the years. It is a cry that was uttered countless millions of times before it became articulate upon Paul's lips. It has been uttered countless millions of times since then. What is this divided man saying? Just this: "O wretched man that I am! who shall deliver me?" It is a cry of sheer agony. It is wet with the tears of frustration and bitter heartache. I read recently of a man in excellent circumstances who committed suicide. The one reason he gave for his rash deed was this, "I am tired of fighting with myself."

3. Then this man being divided and wretched was also antisocial. He had separated himself from his fellows. He lived alone. Nobody could live with him. He was too thoroughly disagreeable. Warring with himself, he also warred with his fellows. And that is the case in some degree with all divided personalities. When we get to fighting with ourselves, we tend to fight with everyone else. When we go to pieces and explode over nothing, when we lose our tempers and slam doors and break up dishes, when we unsheath the sword of our tongue and stab right and left, we call it "nerves." We tell how poorly we slept last night, and how badly we feel. But often the real reason is that we lack inward harmony. We are at war with ourselves. Those torn by inward strife are generally hard to live with.

Being unable to live with his fellows, he was equally unable to live for them. He was, therefore, rendering no high service. He was too busy fighting with himself to have any time for the needs of others. In fact he was a liability rather than an asset, a hindrance rather than a help. Instead of making the burdens of others a bit lighter, he made them the more difficult. Inward conflict always prevents us from enjoying that leisure from ourselves that is necessary to our highest usefulness. In extreme cases, it does for us what it did for this demoniac: makes of us burdens rather than blessings; places us among those who lean rather than among those who lift.

4. Finally, this man was rated as an incurable. He had no hope for himself. Nobody had any hope for him. He was beyond help. "No man," the story says, "could tame him." Thus he was, when Jesus found him, divided, wretched, unable to live with and for his fellows. His is an extreme case, I know, very extreme. But there are few of us that cannot recognize our kinship to him. His needs, therefore, are our needs. What Jesus did for him, is what we long that he should do for us. What Jesus did for him, he surely can do for us. He is still able to save unto the uttermost.

II

Now, what did Jesus do for this demoniac?

1. He gave him a unified personality. That he can do for you and me. And we are not likely to reach

this high goal except through him. Certainly no man can ever find inward peace by yielding to his baser self. However fully he may seem to do so, he can never quite hush the voices that call from the heights. One of the most heartless women of all literature is Lady Macbeth. It would seem that the fiends had heard her prayer when she prayed that they would take her milk for gall. She could turn a loyal husband into a murdering traitor, seemingly without compunction. She could plot the death of a royal guest with devilish eagerness. She seems so utterly bad as to be past feeling. But such was not the case. In her waking moments, by sheer force of will, she could hide the terrible war that raged within. But not so in sleep. Then the conflict reveals itself as she seeks to cleanse her bloody hands, crying, "Out, damned spot! out, I say!"

We find the same truth in Jack London's *The Call of the Wild*—the best dog story, in my opinion, ever written. You remember the hero of the story, a splendid Newfoundland, named Buck. Now Buck was stolen from his home in the States and shipped to Alaska. Here he had to begin life anew. He was no longer a fireside pet. He was in a harsh world where in order to survive he had to learn to live according to the law of the club and fang. He became a husky, the pride of his new master. He was the best and strongest dog that ran the trail. But it came to pass by and by that his master became ill. As a result,

Buck had more leisure than was good for him. In his restlessness, he began to make excursions into the forest. At first these were brief, but gradually they became longer. Soon he was a good hunter, amply able to provide his own food. One night while on a hunt, he heard the howl of a wolf. At once his bristles went up. He was prepared to do battle with this wild thing that he felt was a natural enemy.

But as time went on, and the master continued ill, Buck became accustomed to these weird howls. One night, therefore, when he came face to face with this wolf whose mere howls had once raised his bristles and made him eager for battle, there was no conflict at all. Instead, the dog and the wolf put their noses together in token of the fact that they had buried the hatchet. Together they trotted through the aisles of the forest. Together they sat upon their haunches and howled to the distant stars as their ancestors had done centuries before. But always, with the breaking of the day, Buck would return home. At last, his master died and the big tie that bound him to the old life was broken. Soon after that, Buck began to run with the pack, seemingly the wildest wolf of them all. Yet, I daresay, he could never quite throw off all restraints of his former life. He could never become completely a wolf. Certainly this is true with ourselves. Therefore, to take the lower road is to be a divided personality to the end of the day.

But if we cannot find a unified personality by taking the lower road, we can find it by taking the higher. Here again we are not talking the language of theory, but of experience. Listen, once more, to Paul's anguished cry: "O wretched man that I am! who shall deliver?" Who indeed? Is there a satisfactory answer to that pressing question? There is. Paul answers it out of his own experiences: "I thank God through Jesus Christ." "There is therefore now no condemnation," no inner conflict. He has won as we may win, not by fighting against God, but by surrendering to him. This is what our Lord longs to do for every one of us. He gave and gives to those who fully surrender to him a unified personality.

2. Jesus gave to this tempest-tossed man inward peace. This is ever the result when we make our surrender to God full and complete. For when we have peace with God, we have peace within ourselves. Some years ago, I had a good friend, a minister, who made shipwreck of his faith. But after much inward conflict and much suffering, he turned back to the Christ that he had forsaken. One day in the course of an intimate conversation he told me his experience. "Have you recovered your old joy?" I asked him when the story was ended. "Better than that," he answered, "I have peace." That is our Lord's special legacy to every one of us: "Peace I leave with you, my peace I give unto you." This is one of the great things that Jesus did and does for those who give him a chance. Every

man's religion ought to give him that inward unity that has its issues in inward peace.

3. Jesus enabled this man to live with and for his fellows. He sent him back to the intimate circle of his own family. He sent him to those that we either love the best or hate the most. He sent him back to live with those with whom, till this experience, he could not live. A prominent physician who lives in another city came to see me the other day. He had but one object in his visit and that was to tell me his experience. After lean, gray years, Christ had come into his life. And among the winsome changes that Christ had wrought, this seemed to give him greatest joy, that he had enabled him to rebuild his broken home. And right here is one of the sharpest and highest tests of our religion. Does it make us easy to live with? If we are cantankerous and disagreeable, if everybody is sorry when we come and glad when we go, then however Christian we may think ourselves, we have missed the mark. Here is a test that every man ought to put to his religion: does it enable him to live with his fellows? A real Christian will certainly be able to meet this test.

Not only did Jesus enable this man to live with folks, he also enabled him to live for them. After this experience, this one-time demoniac had enough leisure from himself to care for those to whom he had once been indifferent, to help where he had been only a hindrance. He helped by what he did. He helped even more by what he was. There is no measuring the service that anyone renders, out of whose eyes looks the peace of a great discovery. "Go home," says Luke, "and show how great things the Lord hath done for thee." Show by what you do. Show by what you are.

Stanley Jones tells of a physician who found a stray dog with a broken leg. He took that dog to his home, put the leg in splints, and soon he was able to walk again. Then one day the seemingly ungrateful animal disappeared. The doctor was surprised that after so much kindness the dog should leave him. But he was away for just one night. The next morning there was a scratching at the door. When the doctor opened the door, there was the dog whose leg he had healed. But he was not alone. With him was another dog; lame, as he himself had been, but who had come at the invitation of his friend to be healed. It is as we are gripped by a passion to share that we build up our own personality, and the personalities of others as well.

III

Here, then, are some of the great things that our Lord can do for us. He can give us a unified personality. He can give us inward peace. He can enable us to live with and for our fellows. Of course, we are not claiming that he does all these instantly. But instantly he can make a beginning. How, then, are we to set about the realization of the great things that he longs to do for us?

Our first step is to be converted. That sounds a bit old-fashioned, I know. Conversion is a word that has lost cast among church people in recent years. But if it has lost in one group, it has gained in another. When the teachers and the preachers began to forsake it, then the psychologists took it up. Conversion is a fact. We may be born anew. We can be born from above or from below. I have seen both kinds, and so have you. Sometime ago I met a girl whom I had known in former years as a beautiful and devoted Christian. She had been a life volunteer. But how she had changed! Her face was different. There was a different look in her eyes. She carried herself in a different fashion. Her very walk had a swagger about it that was all but vulgar. What was the matter? She had become the intimate companion of a scoundrel, and in his fellowship she had been reborn, born from below.

But it is our privilege to be born from above. To do this, we must change the master passion of our lives from self to Another. We must become Christ-centered instead of self-centered. When Jesus passed by and said to Matthew, "Follow me," instantly he rose up and followed him. That was Matthew's spiritual birthday. That was his first step toward a unified personality. Why was this the case? Because he had found One whom with deeper and deeper loyalty he could call Master. What did Buck need to steady him when the spell of the wild was upon him? It was not a new kind of collar. It was not a stronger chain. What he needed and all he needed was a master. No dog ever arrives without a master, and this is just as true of a man as of a dog. What do you need with your soul as full of jarring discord as clashing instruments played out of tune? You need a master, The Master. Put the baton into his hands and he will change your discord into winsome music.

"I walked life's way with a careless tread,
I followed where comfort and pleasure led;
Till at last one day in a quiet place,
I met my Master face to face.

I'd reared my castles and built them high,
Till their turrets touched the blue of the sky.
And I'd vowed to rule with an iron mace—
When I met my Master face to face.

I met Him and knew Him and blushed to see
That His eyes in pity were fixed on me,
And I faltered and fell at His feet that day,
And my castles melted and vanished away.

They melted and vanished, and in their place
I saw naught else but the Master's face.
And I cried aloud, 'O make me meet
To follow the path of their bruised feet!'

My care is now for the souls of men.
I've lost my life to find it again,
E'er since that day, in a quiet place,
I met my Master face to face."

XI

THE HIGH ART OF NOT PAYING ATTENTION

"But Jesus paid no attention to what they said."

MARK 5: 36 (GOODSPEED)

"BUT JESUS PAID NO ATTENTION TO WHAT THEY said." How magnificent! What high courage it took to do that! What daring faith! But this was what Jesus was constantly doing. There were always voices clamoring for his attention to which he turned a deaf ear. This is one of the secrets of his victorious life. For instance, there were those who said that the way to win was to be a "go-getter." But Jesus paid no attention to what these said, declaring rather that the meek should inherit the earth. There were multitudes that were contending that the sword was the pathway to power. But Jesus paid no attention to these, knowing that he that takes the sword shall perish by the sword. There were those who warned him earnestly against the cross, but Jesus paid no attention to what they said. He rather accepted the cross in the faith that, lifted up by it, he would draw all men unto himself. Jesus had the high art of not paying attention developed to perfection.

The story of which our text is a part furnishes a striking example of this. A desperate man, Jairus by name, has come to him with a pressing request. He flings himself at the Master's feet and tells him that his little daughter is very ill, that even now she is swinging like a pendulum between life and death; but that there is still hope if he will only make haste to come and lay his hand upon her. Jesus cannot resist this pathetic appeal. At once he turns his face toward the house of suffering, and the heart of the anxious father fairly sings within him for joy. But there is an interruption. Jesus stops to deal with a needy woman who has touched him in the crowd. He is so leisurely about it that the father becomes almost frantic with fear. He can hardly keep from turning in hot anger upon the woman who has appealed to the Master at this inopportune time. "She could have waited," he doubtless says to himself. "But in the case of my child there can be no delay. It is now or never."

Then, what he so desperately fears actually happens. The Master has hardly resumed his journey when messengers come with devastating news. They seem quite officious, these messengers. They delight in telling news. They seem to be of those who would rather tell bad news than to tell none at all. There are those, you know, who would almost be willing to die themselves if they could be privileged to announce their own funerals. "Thy daughter is dead," they announce brutally. "Why trouble the Master any further?" At that the father's hope dies, and his face becomes wet with tears. "Too late," he whispers to himself bitterly. The crowd looks on in sympathetic silence. Perhaps the light even fades from the face of the woman who has just been healed, as she feels that her healing has been bought at too great a price.

But there is One present upon whom this fatal and final news has no effect at all—that is the Master. The same calm assurance looks out from his eyes. There is the same high courage in his voice. He acts in every way just as he would have acted had these messengers of despair never spoken. "Jesus paid no attention to what they said." On the contrary, he turns to the heartbroken father with this word of quiet confidence: "Be not afraid, only believe." Then, instead of apologizing, instead of saying, "I am sorry that I am too late," he continues his errand, never stopping till he has changed death into life, and the house of mourning into the house of laughter and joy. Thus Jesus won because he refused to pay any attention to the prophets of doom.

I

The first word that this story has for us is this: When we set out on any high quest, we, too, may count on meeting with prophets of disaster. There is absolutely no escape. Every Columbus who would discover a new continent must encounter those that will warn him of the futility and madness of his undertaking. Every astronomer that would think God's thoughts after Him must do so amidst the shrieks of those who tell him of the utter hopelessness of his enterprise. Every perfecter of a new invention must transform his dream into reality while the prophets of doom are doing their best to persuade that he cannot succeed. No man ever undertakes anything that is really worth doing but that somebody tells him that all hope of victory is dead, and that the only wise course is to quit and give over his dream.

This morning I am talking to some youth whose heart has been taken captive by Jesus Christ. You are out on the highest of all quests—the quest of Christlike character. You yearn to receive of his fullness. You long that the beauty of the Lord your God shall rest upon you as the sunshine rests upon the hills. You are praying hopefully:

> "O for the man to arise in me,
> That the man I am may cease to be."

And the wonder of it is that yours is an altogether possible achievement. But, I must warn you that there are many voices that speak to the contrary. Some of these voices come out of the past. They are the memories of your failures of yesterday. Some of them come from certain sane and practical folks that look upon Jesus as a dreamer. Others still are the unconscious voices of nominal disciples whose faulty and shabby lives so proclaim their own spiritual poverty as to make Christianity seem either worthless or impossible. Every Pilgrim setting out for the Celestial City, with the cry of "Life, Life, Eternal Life!" upon his lips, is sure to have insistent voices calling after him, and bidding him stay.

The same will be true if you set yourself to render any high and worthful service. Perchance God has put it into your heart to be interested in boys and girls. You have come to believe in the supreme importance of right training. You are convinced that under such training, these young lives will blossom into the knowledge of Jesus Christ as naturally as a rose blooms at the kiss of the springtime. But, there are other voices that seek to upset this brave faith. They tell you that a child must become morally sick before it can be morally well, that it must be lost before it can be found. They affirm that the best equipment for being at home in the Father's house is a sojourn in the far country. They contend that prevention is a rather dull and unexciting something, little worthy of the power of God; that His might is shown at its best, not in prevention, but in cure.

But, while clinging to our faith that our biggest opportunity is with childhood and youth, we must not despair of those who have gone into the far country. Cynical voices, of course, will tell us that the crooked can never be made straight. They will warn us of the utter impossibility of reaching certain damaged souls. A friend pointed out one such to me some time ago. He warned me of the foolishness of speaking to him. I took him at his word till I was practically forced to speak by a combination of circumstances over which I had no control. Then, to my amazement, I found him with a sense of desperate need. I found, also, that his heart was as tender almost as the heart of a child. But I warn you that you will never undertake the introducing of one single soul to Christ but that there will be numerous voices that tell you that you cannot succeed.

Then, there are some who are looking forward to a world where economic injustice shall be done away. You are dreaming of a time when all race hatreds shall be healed. There are those who are even daring to look forward to, and to work toward, a warless world. But, how many voices there are that seek to deter us from dreaming these daring dreams! They wail, "Human nature can never be changed. Man is a savage under his skin and always will be. While there is more talk of a warless world today than in any other time in human history, there were never before such frantic peacetime preparations for war." Thus it is that all who are bent on any high quest must constantly encounter those who tell us that our hope is dead, and that there is no use in making any further effort.

II

What are we to do about this?

1. We can give ear to these prophets of despair. But if we do this, one of two tragic results will doubtless follow. We shall either become half-hearted in our efforts, or quit altogether. Of course to become half-hearted is to fail. A double-minded man is unreliable in all his ways. Years ago, when we were boys, my brother and I were making our way to a certain goal at the back side of our farm. We came to what was normally a rivulet so narrow that one might step across it. But there was a rise in the river, and the flood waters had backed up this little stream until it was now some twelve feet wide. But we would not be turned back. We, therefore, decided to jump across it. I was to jump first. I took a good running start and could have succeeded easily enough, but just before I made the effort my brother changed his mind and shouted, "Stop, stop, stop!" Instead of paying no attention to what he said, I listened to him, with the result that I made a half-hearted jump, and hit right in the middle of the stream. There are many in the Church that are failing in the same fashion. They have not surrendered. They have become half-starved. They are, therefore, possessed of a religion that satisfies neither God nor man.

Then, sometimes these prophets of doom cause us to give over our high quest altogether. There is a significant verse tucked away in the Gospel of St. Mark: "There followed him a certain young man, having a linen cloth cast about his naked body; and the young men laid hold of him and he left the cloth in their hands, and fled from them, naked." It is Thursday evening in Jerusalem. Some Roman soldiers, followed by a mob, are hurrying down one of the narrow streets of the city. In a certain house on that street is a young man who is preparing for bed, or who is just from the bath. He hears the tumult. His curiosity is aroused. He opens the door to a slit and asks what is happening. "We are going out to Gethsemane to arrest Jesus of Nazareth," is the reply. By this news the young man is transformed. He knows Jesus. He has wished to follow him, but possibly has never quite dared. But, now a noble madness is upon him. Not taking time to dress, he grabs a sheet and wraps it about his body, and flees into the night to die, if need be, by the side of Jesus. But something happens to break the spell. He runs into a group of young fellows who see the madness of his high quest. He comes to himself, leaves the cloth in their hands, and flees naked into the night. His tragedy was that he paid attention to the wrong voices.

This is the case with entirely too many today. That was a pathetic wail that a certain group of ministers sent out the other day. They proclaimed the utter bankruptcy of Protestantism, and warned that our one hope was to flee to Rome for refuge. Of course this does not mean that what they said is true. It only means that these have been so attentive to the prophets of despair that they have become unmanned, and have given over the fight. This is also the tragic plight of not a few in the pew. Some time ago a layman said in my presence, "The devil has my church, therefore I am not going any more." But a robust old saint, who belonged to the same church, answered, "He may have your pew—I never see you in it; but he hasn't mine yet. I occupy it every Sunday." The trouble with this quitter was that he had failed to cultivate the high art of not paying attention.

2. But we may follow the example of our Lord and pay no attention to these sad wails. That has been the method of every man that has ever made a success of any worthy enterprise. When as a young chap I was preparing to get married, I confided the good news to a few of my mature friends. I expected their faces to light up and their eyes to sparkle. But, to my amazement, this did not happen. For the most part they merely looked sad and undertook to warn me of the risk I was running. But, thank God, I paid no attention to what they said. A man told me recently, with a voice of despair, that with the depression, and with the death of so many of our older members, our church was headed for the rocks. But instead of bursting into tears and getting ready to move, I paid absolutely no attention to him. This is a habit I have

tried, with some degree of success, to cultivate throughout my ministry.

I had to begin this habit early. After I had been preaching for only five months I was sent to follow a pastor who had been distressingly popular. The congregation was angry at him for leaving and at me for coming. Soon after my arrival, a gentleman came with this pleasing announcement: "Mr. A. is going to quit this church." "Why?" I asked. "Because you are not big enough for the job, and he is not going to stay here and see it topple about his ears." A few days later another came with a similar message with regard to Mr. B. Then, another with regard to Mr. C. Being quite young, I had an idea that these ought to help all the more since things were so shaky. But they did not think so, and I was naturally greatly distressed. But even a worm will turn sometimes. So, after listening to these voices of doom for some six weeks I decided to quit it. The next Sunday I stepped into my pulpit, held up some paper, and said: "All who desire to leave this church because it is dying may have their certificates at the close of this service."

Then, I continued: "This week I witnessed a scene that heartened me greatly. I saw a man buy a bottle of soda pop. (It was one of the old-fashioned kind that opened with a loud noise, a bit like the report of a revolver.) When he had uncorked it, it began to splutter and bubble furiously. I could hardly keep from shouting at the fellow, though he was a stranger,

'Drink it, man, drink it, else you will lose every drop of it.' But he waited and watched with placid indifference. By and by it grew quiet. Then I looked, and, to my amazement, the bottle seemed just as full as at the beginning. Nothing had escaped but a few bubbles and a little wind. 'Now,' I said, 'you bubbles and wind, come and get your letters.'" And not one came, and the situation was saved. There are always those who wail, but we can refuse to listen.

III

But how can we help paying attention? How did Jesus do it? He did not do so by merely stopping his ears. There are those who seek to silence these clamorous voices by a monkish withdrawal from the world. That is entirely futile. If you have a radio, you can keep it turned off and thereby refuse to hear anything objectionable. But, in that case, your radio is entirely useless. The better way is to tune out the worthless by tuning in the worthful. The air is full of voices. You can hear the choicest of arias, if you desire. But, if your taste runs in another direction, you can listen to that masterpiece, "The Music Goes Round and Round." The air is also full of voices that call to faith and courage and of voices that call to doubt and despair. In the old Genesis story, we read, "God said," and we read, also, "The serpent said." God is still broadcasting, and so is the serpent. It is our high privilege to tune in on God and thereby hush these lower voices into silence. This has been the way of the saints through all the centuries.

Take Abraham, for example. You will notice that when the writers of the New Testament want to tell us what religion is at its best they keep turning back to this strange old hero, who left Ur of the Chaldees at God's call to journey into the unknown. He was lured on by the promise that he should become the father of a great nation. But the swift years slipped by, and nothing came of it. Now, he is an old man, and Sarah has passed from life's springtime into withered winter. How the devastations that the years have wrought shriek at him! How insistently they say, "Look at your age-worn body, and see how impossible your dream is." But Abraham paid no attention to what they said. He was too intent upon the voice of God. "He considered not his own body, now dead . . . but was strong in faith, giving glory to God, being fully persuaded that what He had promised, He was able also to perform."

Some years ago one of my dearest friends, who increased the loveliness of heaven recently by passing into it, told me this intimate and personal experience. He did not tell it in public. He was a man of beautiful spiritual modesty. "Once," he said, "my little girl was desperately ill with membranous croup. Late one afternoon I lifted her into my arms to rest her a bit. She looked pathetically into my face and said: 'Daddy, am I going to get well?' 'Darling,' I answered, 'Daddy doesn't know. I am hoping that you will.' Then," he continued, "it came to me that I might know, for there was One willing to tell me. I then gave her into the arms of the nurse and hurried to my place of prayer. I did not ask for the life of my child; I only asked to know the will of God in the matter. As I prayed I became sure that she was going to recover. I hurried home to tell my wife the good news. The night came on, we went to bed as usual, and I was soon asleep. How long I slept, I do not know. But when I awoke my wife and the nurse were bending over the baby's bed, and I heard the mother say, 'Is she dead?' " Now, there was a test. What did this man do who had gone to sleep so sure of the recovery of his child? Did he spring from bed frantic with fear? Did he conclude at once that God had let him down? That question, "Is she dead?"—no voice could have been more disconcerting than that. But this strong saint turned his face to the wall without a word and went back to sleep. In other words, when doubt and despair clamored for his attention, he paid no attention to what they said. The next morning, he learned the reason for the mother's question. The child had been breathing so quietly that she feared she was not breathing at all. But what she had taken for death was in reality the return of life.

"Faith, mighty faith, the promise sees,
  And looks to God alone;
Laughs at impossibilities,
  And cries, 'It shall be done.' "

Healing the Woman with the Issue of Blood

XII

HOW TO TALK TO YOURSELF

"What she said to herself was this . . ."

MATTHEW 9: 21 (MOFFATT)

I

HERE IS A WOMAN WHO IS HAVING A CONVERSATION with herself. We all do that at times, and what we say to ourselves is vastly important. Of course, we recognize how tremendously we are influenced by the words of others. A wrong word has often meant the utter marring of a life. Many a child foolishly rebuked for stupidity, for instance, by a parent or a teacher has gone out under that influence to a lifelong battle with an inferiority complex. Words of abuse have so convinced many another child of his badness, that, in utter discouragement, he has gone to a life of wrongdoing, and, at times, to one of positive crime. There is, in fact, no measuring the possible harm of one wrong word.

But if wrong words can do endless harm, right words can do endless good. "A word fitly spoken," said a wise man, "is like apples of gold in pictures of silver." There are words that have power to grip us by the shoulder and shake us out of our sleep, power to turn indifference into wide-eyed awareness. There are words that tell us of the hidden gold that is in our own undeveloped personalities. There are words that have skill to break up the drought of the soul and set the fields of the heart to flowering. I am thinking of a man now, a successful minister, who as a boy was so careless and indifferent that he was all but the despair of his family. But when tragedy came into the home in the death of his father, Jim chanced to overhear an older brother comforting and encouraging his mother. It so happened that the word he overheard, not meant for his own ears, ran something like this, "You can count on Jim. He is gifted. He will certainly make something some day." And Jim thinks with gratitude of that word to this day. It thrilled him like a trumpet call, and sent him out with a keen zest for battle.

Then when things have gone wrong and life has crashed into ruins, how much the word of a friend can often do for us! When we walk in slippery places, when we need a strong staff upon which to lean, when we need a sturdy something against which to lean our backs, we find that something oftentimes to be a word fitly spoken. "Your words have kept men on their feet," was a compliment, a rather grudging compliment I think, to Job from one of his comforters. Few bigger things than that could be said about any man.

We ought to be exceedingly careful what we say to each other, for our words have power to hurt or power to help. They have power to kill or power to make alive. It is next to impossible to overestimate their might for weal or for woe.

But, if what we say to each other is important, what we say to ourselves is even more important. Tell me what you habitually say to yourself, and I will tell you the kind of man you are. Tell me what you say to yourself, and I will tell you what you are likely to become. Take the Rich Farmer of whom Jesus spoke, for instance. He was a successful man, honorable and upright. No doubt, he was a pillar in church and state. But how little his neighbors really knew about him! We should never have known him at all if we had not overheard a conversation that he had with himself. If we had only overheard him talking to his minister, we might not have known him. If we listened as he talked to his wife, we might still have been in doubt. But when we hear him as he talks to himself, we know him for what he is.

Listen to him! He is looking out over a fertile farm that is growing golden with abundant harvest. The rain and the sunshine have come in just the right proportions. He himself has enjoyed excellent health. His fellow-workers have been energetic and faithful. Therefore, as he looks over his bumper crops that are far beyond his own needs, he begins to talk to himself. As we listen, we naturally expect him to say something like this: "God has been most gracious to me. Those who have been in my employ have been very faithful. I have made far more than I need. Out of sheer gratitude, I am eager to use some of this abundant harvest for the common good."

But unfortunately, that is not what he said. As we listen to him, we learn that he has no slightest appreciation of the help of either God or man. He has no sense of obligation. His one thought is how he can conserve all his wealth for himself. He knows no better bank in which to deposit his gains than a barn. "I will pull down my barns, and build greater; and there will I bestow all my fruits and my goods. And I will say to my soul, Soul, thou hast much goods laid up for many years; eat, drink, have a good time." It was by such talk as this that he showed himself to be an utter fool, a pathetic moral imbecile, with no more appreciation of life's finer values than a pig would have for a sunrise. We know him for what he is by what he said to himself.

II

Now what did this woman say to herself? She might have said some very distressing things, and have told the strictest truth. Life had dealt very harshly with her. In the springtime of her years, she had become the victim of a shamefaced disease. It was a disease that made her morally unclean. It was a disease that had robbed her of almost every worthy prize.

It had robbed her of about the only vocation open to women in that day—the vocation of wifehood and motherhood. This heavy handicap seems to have been softened in some measure, at the beginning, by the fact that she was a woman of independent means. But she was a resolute woman. When her sickness came upon her, she determined that she would not die without a fight. If there was any cure to be had, she would have it. Therefore, for twelve long years she went to one physician after another. But these relieved her of nothing but her money. Today she is a little more faded, a little more weak, a little nearer the cemetery than ever before. And to the burden of her sickness has now been added the burden of poverty.

How easy, under these circumstances, it would have been for her to have had a grudge against life. "I am suffering," she might have told herself, "and that through no fault of my own. I have not been a coward. I have tried hard to be well. I have spent my very all. But there is no hope. The cards are stacked against me. Life has cheated me. I no longer believe that there is a good God back of the universe. If there were, He could not allow me to suffer so deeply and so needlessly." This would have been an easy conversation for this woman. But if she had talked to herself in this fashion, she would either have sunk into hopeless invalidism, or have chucked the whole business and jumped out the window.

What then did she say? She said: "I am sick, it is

true, but I am not dead yet. I have seemingly exhausted all of my resources, but that is not exactly the case. A new Personality has come upon the horizon, Jesus by name. They tell me that his hands have cunning to work cures that none other can work. I have heard that the very might of God is in him. Maybe he can help me. At least I am going to try him. I am going to him with the conviction that if I do my part, he will do his. If I win, I win. If I fail, after having done my best, I shall certainly not be any worse off than I am. But I will not fail. If I touch but the tassel of his robe, I shall be healed." Thus this brave woman talked to herself.

III

Now what was the outcome of this daring conversation?

1. By thus talking to herself, she kept alive her hope. By thus talking to herself, she kept her courage from dying utterly. Of course, you know that when we lose heart and hope, we are through. If you think you are licked, you are. If you believe you are whipped, then you are whipped. If you have been knocked down flat and have convinced yourself that you can never get up, you are likely to lie there and whine the rest of your days. If you have made up your mind to die, then die you will, in spite of all that physicians can do for you. But no man is ever quite beyond the possibility of help till he concedes defeat within his

own soul. This woman talked to herself in such a fashion as to keep alive her courage and hope.

2. By keeping up her hope, she was able to keep up the struggle. When we lose hope, we stop trying. That is true in every department of human endeavor. Tell yourself you cannot hold your job, and you are likely to quit even trying to hold it. Tell yourself that you can never be well, and you will give over the fight for health. Tell yourself that the life abundant is not for you, that all Christ's wealthy promises are but empty nothings so far as you are concerned, and your soul will forget its high quest and accept failure without a struggle. There are multitudes today who no longer make any serious effort at being Christians, not because Christlikeness no longer appeals to them, but because its attainment seems so impossible. But as long as we hope, we can keep up the struggle.

One day, therefore, when the exciting news is brought that Jesus is in her neighborhood, she resolves to go to him. But she meets with difficulties. Multitudes of curious people are thronging him. They are not crusaders. They are just vagrants. They are, therefore, in the way. But in the face of opposition, she keeps encouraging herself with this word, "If I may touch but his clothes, I shall be healed." So she struggles on till at last her finger touches the tassel of his robe. At once she is healed—not by her finger, but by her faith. Thus by talking to herself in terms of faith, she finds the bodily healing for which she seeks. Not only so, but she finds what is far more priceless, healing of heart. As she kneels at the Master's feet, he bids her go in peace.

IV

Now, what are we saying to ourselves? Some of us are talking to ourselves in a fashion that makes only for our weakening.

There are those, for instance, who are soothing themselves by enervating alibis. Perhaps you are conscious of the fact that you have not played the game very well. You have been untrue to your convictions. You have flung away your former ideals. You have chucked your moral standards. You can be at home today in a companionship that once would have disgusted you. You have learned to take on the color of your crowd as readily as a chameleon. "It is true that I drank a bit at the party the other night. It is true also that I have pronounced convictions against drinking. But everybody else drank, therefore I went with the crowd. What else could I do? Surely you could not expect me to be peculiar. I played the weakling and the fool, but it was not my fault. It was the best I could do under the circumstances." Thus, some of us weaken ourselves by soft alibis.

Then, others of us weaken ourselves by baby talk. Life has dealt us some rather hefty blows. We have not had as good opportunities as some of our friends. We have handicaps that it seems impossible for us to overcome. Therefore, we tell ourselves that we are pitiable creatures, shut out from any possibility of playing the game well. If we only had a better chance, we should doubtless do big things. But under the circumstances, anything worthwhile is impossible. Therefore, we coddle ourselves and kill our possibilities by self-pity. This we do, while all about us are those in far worse circumstances who are fighting their way to victory.

Then there are not a few who talk themselves into doubt, and even into positive unbelief. A certain psalmist knew a man of this kind. God became an embarrassment to him. Just as a son of the parsonage who is going wrong is often angered by being reminded that he is a minister's son, so this man was angered and annoyed by being reminded, even by himself, that he was a son of the Most High. The fact of such a relationship laid demands upon him that he was unwilling to meet. He came to see with increasing clearness that he had either to get rid of God or give up the selfish life that he was living. Lacking the courage to change, he decided to ditch God.

And how did he go about it? Just as millions of others have done. He had a conversation with himself. He told himself frankly that God did not exist. "The fool hath said in his heart," that is to himself, "there is no God." Having gotten rid of God, he continued his conversation to its inevitable conclusion: "Since there is no God, I am not really a child of the King.

I am the product of blind forces that had no prevision of what they were creating. I am a child of the mud. I can now go my own filthy way and still be quite worthy of such a sire. Thus not a few, lacking the courage to live up to the demands of a vital faith, talk themselves into unbelief.

But if it is possible to talk ourselves toward defeat, it is also possible to talk ourselves toward victory. If you can lessen your chances of health by forever telling yourself that you are sick, so you can help yourself toward health by talking encouragingly to yourself. This is especially true of nervous diseases. I knew a man some years ago who had a bad nervous breakdown. Now the psychologists tell us that all such breakdowns are subconsciously desired. That is, we get into a hard situation where we tell ourselves that there is no good way out but to get sick. Then we proceed to act accordingly. Be that as it may, such sickness is a most depressing experience. Our nerves are good liars. They tell us all sorts of horrible stories: That we have not slept, even when we have, and will never sleep again; that we are the greatest sufferers in the world, and always will be. So it was with this gentleman: once sunny, he became about as cheerful as a dust storm.

But one day he took himself in hand. He told himself plainly that something had to be done, and that he was the one to do it. "You are going to quit moping about, looking like a chicken with a bad case of cholera," he told himself; "you are going to brace up and get well." And, as Ripley would say, "believe it or not," he began from that day to improve. Soon he was enjoying vigorous health. Of course, this would not work with every kind of sickness, but I doubt if there is any that it would not improve. Then, too, such a course would make it easier for the sick body to live with himself. It would also make it easier for others to live with him.

Now, if talking to ourselves aright is a help toward physical recovery, it is certainly not less so in the realm of the moral and spiritual. You remember that tenderly beautiful story that Jesus told. It is of the graceless laddie who went away from home. This boy was eager to be on his own. He desired to get some place where he could be independent of his father. So he went into a far country. Here he ran through with his wealth and came down to utter poverty. He had to go out seeking for a job, and the best that he could find was the herding of a bunch of swine. The whole adventure had proved bitterly disappointing. And now, we find him in the hogpen, having a talk with himself. Let us draw near and hear what he has to say. His conversation might have run something like this:

"My father is a graceless old fossil. The mess I am in is all his fault. He ought to have refused to have given me my share of goods. He might have known that something like this would happen. Why did God make it possible for a man to sin anyway? Why did He give us the power of choice? Of course, I know that the price a man pays for the capacity to climb is his capacity to go down; that if he is capable of doing right, he must also be capable of doing wrong. If he has the possibilities of heaven in him, he must also have the possibilities of hell. But while I can't think of a better way, this one is all wrong. Then there is that brother of mine, cold as ice and hard as nails. I might never have left home but for him. And what fine friends I've had! They helped me spend my money, then threw me to the hogs. Everybody has played me false. Therefore, I am just going to lie down and die. Then they'll all be sorry they treated me as they have."

Many a man has talked to himself after this fashion, and, thus talking, has slipped into the pit. But this prodigal did infinitely better. What really did he say? Listen: When he came to himself, he said: "I was an awful fool to have left my father as I did. But it was my own choice. I have nobody to blame but myself. I thought I was going to have a great time down here. I looked forward to an endless round of feasts. But what I have really found is hunger to the point of starvation. Now, though my friends have thrown me down, and though my brother will likely not give me welcome, I am going back. There is one who will welcome me. He has the tenderest of hearts. His very servants have bread enough and to spare. He will not refuse me, unworthy as I am, for I am his son. Therefore, I am going to rise and go to my father. I am going openly. I left openly. I am going back the same way. I am not going to spare myself. And when I get back, I am going to tell my father the plain truth, just as I am now telling it to myself."

That wholesome conversation got action. Having thus told himself the truth, he picked himself up and turned his face toward home. And you know the happy ending: "When he was yet a great way off, his father saw him and had compassion on him, and ran and fell on his neck and kissed him." Then his father gave him the best robe and the best possible feast and the best possible home. He gave him also, not the place of a servant, but of a son. And so God will do for us, if we will tell ourselves the truth about ourselves, and act accordingly. He is our Father and is eager to give us his best. Frankly face your own spiritual poverty. But as you do so, face the further fact that you may be rich. Tell yourself that He that spared not His own Son, but delivered him up for us all, will also with him freely give us all things. Thus talking to yourself, you, too, will find a place at the feast of the fullness of life.

Feeding the Five Thousand

XIII

OVERSTATING OUR POVERTY

"We have here but five loaves, and two fishes."

MATTHEW 14: 17

THESE DISCIPLES ARE OBVIOUSLY WORRIED. THEY have come out to this lakeside for a bit of rest. They have come hoping for a little private picnic with their Master. But their hopes were doomed to disappointment. The keel of their boat has hardly touched the shore before they begin to be besieged by a great multitude of troublesome people. These take up all their Master's time, so that they have not a single moment alone with him. The hours are hectic and toilsome, even beyond the ordinary. At last, the shadows are lengthening and the day is almost over. Still these troublesome creatures refuse to leave. By this time, they have become a serious problem. Having been all day without food, they are hungry. But there is no bread to be had in this lonely spot. Besides, if there were, these disciples have no money with which to buy.

Then, to make matters worse, Jesus seems entirely

unconscious of their plight. He is so busy with his teaching that he seems to have forgotten where he is. He is so taken up with the work of healing that he has lost all track of time. They love this Master of theirs. They have no end of admiration for him. But they do not quite trust him. They feel that he requires a good bit of managing. In fact, at present he is more of a liability than an asset. Therefore, there is nothing for them to do but to take matters into their own hands and make the best of a hard situation.

I

Now this is a very human story. It is also very modern. It belongs not simply to a far-off yesterday, it belongs also to today. Life is constantly bringing us both as individuals and as groups into trying and perplexing situations. Again and again we come to veils through which we cannot see and doors to which we find no key. Over and over we are met by demands for which our resources seem entirely inadequate. Some of us are facing such trying situations even now. And, sad to say, our religion does not seem to be doing very much for us. Even our Lord appears to be either totally unmindful of our pathetic plight, or as inadequate to its demands as ourselves. We, as these disciples, feel that the whole burden must rest upon our shoulders and ours alone. No wonder, therefore, we are worried. But what are we to do about it? What did these disciples resolve to do? They resolved to escape. That was a resolution that had in it very little heroism, and none too much good sense. But it is one that we ourselves have tried again and again. We seek to escape by various methods.

1. We employ that of these disciples. They simply stood from under. They "passed the buck." "Send the multitude away," they ordered. "Whatever is done for these hungry men and women will have to be done by somebody else." How familiar that is! There are thousands in this city, for instance, who believe in the Church, who are altogether friendly to it, who would not think of living where there were no churches. But what do they do about it? Naked nothing. They simply stand from under. They allow all the responsibility for their support to rest upon other shoulders. We want a clean city, a wholesome place for our boys and girls to grow to manhood and womanhood. But we refuse to take any part of the responsibility for building such a city.

What a human story is that in the second book of Kings! A small boy has gone out into the field to be with his father. It is harvest time and the day is hot. The blazing sun is too much for the boy. He becomes desperately ill. In his agony, he hurries to his father, crying, "My head, my head." Now, what does this father do? Does he gather him in his arms and do his best to minister to him? Not at all. He does what too many busy fathers have done through the centuries. He "passes the buck." "Take him," he says, "to his mother." But it is not fathers alone who take this cowardly and selfish course. There are multitudes, both men and women, who are seeking to meet their trying situations by simply shirking them or putting the responsibility upon others.

2. Then there are those who seek to escape their hard situations by running. There was a psalmist once who found himself in a situation that literally bristled with difficulties. Old friends had proven unfaithful. Treachery stalked abroad. War and rebellion were in the land. He was sorely troubled. Then he saw a dove rise on swift wings and fly away into the far-flung vault of blue. He watched her as she became first a speck and then faded into utter nothingness. Then he wiped his eyes that had grown moist, partly from looking upon the brightness without, but more from looking upon the darkness within, and he muttered something to himself through lips that were white and drawn with pain. What was he saying? This: "I wish I had wings like a dove. How soon would I fly away and be at rest."

How many have felt like that! There was a certain preacher named Jeremiah who had an appointment that he did not like. His congregation almost drove him to desperation. But one day he thought of a possible remedy. "I wish," he said, "I had a lodging place in the wilderness for wayfaring men, that I might leave my people and go from them." There was another prophet who was appointed to Nineveh, but just as Jeremiah, he did not like his appointment. Therefore, he resolved to run away: "Jonah rose up to flee unto Tarshish from the presence of the Lord." Faced by demands that they felt themselves unable or unwilling to meet, these prophets wanted to escape by running.

But this desire to run is by no means confined to the prophets. We have all felt it. A member of my church, who was having more domestic difficulties than he knew what to do with, said, "My best friend is my hat. Whenever things get too stormy at home, I seize my hat and make my escape." There is a tragically large number who are trying to escape their domestic difficulties by running even to the divorce court. But to run off from a situation just because it is hard is always cowardly, and often futile. This is the case because the trouble from which we are flying is often within ourselves. Of course, we cannot escape that by running. We take it with us. Milton's Satan found that out:

> "Infinite woe and infinite despair:
> Which way I fly is hell; myself am hell!"

3. Then there are those who in their eagerness to escape fling out of life altogether. We have about 22,000 suicides in this country every year. Why do these take this desperate course? Why do they thus dare to quit before the whistle blows? It is generally because they find themselves face to face with trying

situations to which they feel inadequate. They are met by problems they have not the gallantry to try to solve. Of course, as a matter of fact, there are always tens of thousands in situations just as trying as theirs who go bravely forward. Challenged by stark impossibilities, they refuse to surrender, but see the battle through with honor. These, therefore, who slip out of life by the back door do so, not because they must, but because they have not the heroism to face their trying task. Suicide is for them a way of escape from a situation that they have not the gallantry to meet.

II

Why did these disciples seek to escape? It was not because they were altogether selfish. It was not because they were entirely indifferent to the needs of this hungry crowd. They were not indifferent. They were genuinely concerned. No more did they seek to escape because they felt that the physical needs of this multitude were no business of theirs. They were not among those who believe that the one concern of the Church is the spiritual needs of their fellows. Why then, I repeat, did they undertake to send these hungry folks away to shift for themselves? There is but one answer. It was because they felt that there was nothing else to do. There was no other way out. They were plain, practical men, not fanatical dreamers. Therefore, there was nothing to do but to face the ugly facts in the case and act accordingly.

Now what were the facts? When they found themselves face to face with this hungry crowd, with commendable sanity they took account of their resources. Upon so doing, they found those resources entirely inadequate. Then, with a stupidity that has a striking resemblance to good sense, they brought in the following report: "Having made a thorough canvass of our assets, we find that we have but five loaves and two fishes." Having thus faced their pathetic poverty, they quite naturally proceeded to pass the following resolution: "Whereas we are in a desperate situation to which we are entirely inadequate, be it resolved that there is but one sane course open to us, and that is to send the multitude away." How modern it is! It is quite evident that these disciples, though willing to serve, were at once hopeless and helpless in the presence of the pressing demands of the hour.

Why was this the case? It was because they had so grossly overestimated their poverty. "We have here," they said, "but five loaves and two fishes." "Really, is that all?" it seems someone would have asked. "Does that sum up *all* your resources? Do you have no wealth at all except these five loaves and two little dried fish?" "That is all," they answer stupidly. "But how about your Lord and Master?" this questioner might have persisted. "Has he ever failed you? Has he ever let you down? Is it not possible that he might enable you to see this desperate situation through with honor? Instead of looking solely at your material wealth, why not look to him of whom it is written, 'He shall not fail nor be discouraged'?" But they, refusing to reckon with their matchless Master, headed toward utter defeat.

Now, I am convinced that this brings us face to face with the greatest weakness of the modern church. We have far saner views of the Bible than our fathers had. I believe we have a clearer conception of what Jesus is trying to do in our world. I am convinced that our beliefs, for the most part, are more intellectually respectable. But in spite of this, we are sadly lacking in dynamic. Intellectually sane, we are often morally and spiritually impotent. In our efforts to preach to the scientific mind, we have been frightened to death of anything that smacks of the supernatural. Sometimes, therefore, we have left God out altogether. Even when we have suffered Him to remain in the picture, we have too often conceived of Him as so imprisoned in His own universe as to be all but powerless. Now, "Men are like the Gods they serve," Carlyle tells us. A mighty God makes mighty men. But our God is not vastly able, therefore our power is anything but impressive.

How up-to-date is this old story! The prophet Elisha has a price on his head. He is now spending the night in the city of Dothan. While the city sleeps, a hostile army surrounds it. The one purpose of this army is to capture the prophet. Now Elisha's servant is totally unaware of their danger. When, therefore, he goes out in the morning and discovers that an army is encircling them, he is overcome with fear and despair. "Alas, my master," he cries desperately; "how shall we do?" At once the prophet begins to pray. But he does not pray for deliverance as this servant expects him to do. He rather prays that the eyes of this frightened servant might be opened. When that prayer was answered, when this timid man comes to realize something of the infinite resources of God, his fear gives way to faith and courage. So it was for these disciples when they realized that they did not have to meet this trying situation alone. This day, that seemed destined to end in defeat, ended in victory.

III

How did it come about? The difference was made by their Lord. He was the way out for them, as he is for us. Behold the difference that he makes!

1. These disciples discovered with amazement that their Master had a plan. "Himself knew what he would do," John tells us. How heartening! Then this emergency has not taken him by surprise. He is neither frightened nor worried by it. He has foreseen it and made his plans for meeting it. Therefore, the whole responsibility is not on their weak shoulders. It is on the shoulders of One infinitely wise and infinitely able. Now, this heartening realization is needed by ourselves. We, too, need to know that God has a plan for His world. He has neither forgotten nor

forsaken it. He is now in the midst of it, moving to meet its desperate needs. He will never give over till the kingdoms of the world have become the Kingdoms of our Lord and His Christ.

Not only are we to believe that God has a plan for His world, we are also to believe that He has a plan for each individual soul. Horace Bushnell preached a sermon years ago on the subject, "Every Life a Plan of God." A better statement of the case would possibly be "God Plans Every Life." "As the Father hath sent me into the world," said Jesus, "even so send I you into the world." This does not mean, of course, that God has fixed a certain groove in which we are to run whether we are willing or not. We can thwart God's plan for our lives if we so desire. It simply means that He is the Architect and we are the builders. He makes the plan; we are to execute that plan. To do this, to fulfill God's plan in our lives, is the ultimate in victorious living.

2. Not only did these disciples discover that their Master had a plan and a program for the situation, they discovered also that his was a positive and constructive plan. When these disciples made their plan, it was purely negative. They sought only to send the multitude away—to stand from under. "This situation is bad, therefore we must get out of it," they said. But, that is not our Lord's way. He rather says, "The situation is bad, therefore change it; make it over into what it ought to be." In spite of this, there are many

good people today who believe that God has no better plan for the saving of this world than deserting it. They believe that things are going from bad to worse till they become utterly and hopelessly rotten. Then the Lord will rapture away the little handful of saints that may yet remain, and leave the world to welter in its own ruin. That seems to me to be pessimism at its worst. Our Lord is not here to desert, but to save.

That also is the reason for our being here. Years ago, when I was a teacher in a certain town, I undertook to establish a public library. My first move was to invite my old teacher, Sawney Webb, to deliver a lecture in the opera house. By charging a small admission, I was sure I could get the first few hundred dollars for this undertaking. I advertised thoroughly and looked toward the big event with high hopes. But I was doomed to disappointment. The audience was shamefully small. As we were going back to the hotel after the lecture, I was bewailing the lack of interest in matters worthwhile on the part of the people. But my wise old teacher made this reply: "Son, if everybody were just as they should be, and every situation just as it ought to be, the Lord wouldn't need you and me. But because they are not, that is the reason that we are here." "I pray not," said Jesus, "that thou shouldst take them out of the world." It is not ours to run away; it is ours to stand in our place and thus change our moral doubts into positive convictions.

Our Lord not only calls upon us to do this, but he

makes us equal to the task. "They need not depart," said Jesus. This was the case for at least two reasons: First, because Jesus was present and fully adequate to the situation. He always is. "He is the same yesterday, today, and forever." He is able now as then to supply every need of ours. Then, "they need not depart," because there was no hope elsewhere. And that holds true still. If Christ has not the answer for our bewildered day, then there is no answer. If he cannot show us the way out as individuals and as a world, then there is none who can. All schemes for human betterment that leave him out of consideration are doomed to disappointment. Multitudes, both within and without the Church, are today coming to realize that there is none other Name under heaven given among men whereby we must be saved.

3. These disciples came to understand the simplicity of Jesus' method. The needs of this multitude were met. "All ate and had enough," the story tells us. How was it brought about? It was not brought about by Jesus alone. No more was it brought about by the disciples alone. It was brought about by Jesus and his disciples working together. That is how all great tasks are accomplished. When Paul was explaining how Christianity was sweeping over the Roman world, he used these words: "I planted, Apollos watered; but it was God who made it grow." That is, the Kingdom of God is to come, a new world is to be made, by God and man working together.

This means, of course, that in the making of this new world God is dependent upon man. He walks to His missions upon human feet. He ministers through human hands. He speaks His message through human lips. If anything, therefore, is to be done in our day toward the saving of our humanity, if anything is to be done toward building a better home life, a stronger and more spiritual church life, a more just social order, we are the ones that are going to have to do it. He is the vine, we are the branches. The vine has no way of bearing fruit except through the branches. That simply means that God has no way of bringing in His Kingdom except through you and me. He is absolutely dependent upon ourselves.

But if this is true, it is certainly equally true that we are absolutely dependent upon God. How strangely prone we are to forget this! How prone we are to take the whole task of building a new world upon ourselves, and leaving God out altogether. This is the reason that so many of us are tired, weak, and discouraged. We fret and strain in our own strength and make little progress. But such need not be the case. All the while, God is saying to us, "It is not by might, nor by power, but by my Spirit, saith the Lord." "Ye shall receive power, after that the Holy Spirit is come upon you." "I will give you a mouth and wisdom that men cannot gainsay nor resist." Through our very failures, he keeps impressing upon us this truth:

"Apart from me ye can do nothing." We are absolutely dependent upon God.

What, then, is our present duty, our high privilege? Instead of bewailing our poverty as did these disciples, instead of taking account only of our material resources, we are to take account also of those that are spiritual. We are to count upon God and to co-operate with Him. This we are to do by putting what we have, whether large or small, into His hands. We are to give Him our all—our very selves. This, and this alone, will bring us victory. For, if we give God ourselves, He will accept us. This is true regardless of how weak and futile we may be. If we give Him ourselves, He will cleanse us and fill us with His Spirit. If we give Him ourselves, He will use us for the accomplishment of His purpose. This is not theory; it is experience. "In him who strengthens me," shouts Paul, "I am able for everything." To that tremendous assertion the choicest of the saints say, "Amen." Such a rich experience may be yours and mine. May we begin entering upon it even now!

Peter's Adventure on the Water

XIV
SURVEYING THE WIND

"But when he saw the wind, he was afraid; and beginning to sink, he cried, saying, Lord, save me."

MATTHEW 14: 30

"BEGINNING TO SINK . . ." THAT IS AN ARRESTING and tragic word. A few moments ago Simon Peter was daring the impossible. With the rude winds pounding him, with an enraged sea spitting its spray into his face, he was climbing down out of the boat to go to Jesus. "Lord, if it be thou," he had prayed, "bid me come unto thee on the water." And Jesus, instead of reminding him that he was in sufficiently great danger where he was, granted his request. "Come," he invited. At once, with the light of a great faith in his eyes, Peter planted his feet on that word "Come," and began to walk on the water to go to Jesus. But his success proved to be short-lived. Soon his faith had changed to fear, his victory to defeat. He is beginning to sink. Unless a hand is stretched forth to help him, he will soon be at the bottom of the sea.

I

Now it seems to me that this sinking man is a picture of much that we see in our modern world.

It is a description of many of ourselves. We are not living as victoriously as we once dreamed that we should. While we have not given over the fight, have not wholly surrendered, still we do not seem to be getting anywhere. There are even those who have quit trying. One such came to see me a few days ago. He told me with frank desperation that all of his inner and outer resources had broken down, that he had completely lost his grip. According to his own confession, he was not simply sinking, he had already gone down and the waters of utter defeat were rolling over him.

This sinking man reminds us also of much that we see in our churches. It is at times hard for us to sing "Like a mighty army moves the Church of God" without a sense of unreality. When we realize the terrific moral slump that has overtaken our church life in recent years, we feel that the only army that we greatly resemble is one that is disorganized and discouraged and in retreat. Too often our services are pervaded by an atmosphere of defeat rather than of victory. Many of our churches are more conspicuous for their empty pews than for their growing and enthusiastic congregations. Now, I believe that the worst is over and that the present trend is upward. But in spite of this fact, the average church still reminds us more of one who is sinking than one who is moving victoriously forward on a mission of conquest.

Then what is true of the individual and of the church seems equally true of civilization as a whole. A few years ago we were very sure of ourselves. Just before the outbreak of the World War, we thought we had won the fight and had planted our feet firmly upon the road of an inevitable progress. But all that has changed. Today there is widespread pessimism regarding the future. Every great nation of the world is girding itself for war. The nations of Europe and Asia are threatening at any moment to be at each other's throats. If any two of these nations fight, the chances are that the conflict will be world-wide. Many thoughtful people believe that we cannot bear the strain of another World War. There is, therefore, widespread fear that our present civilization is even now on the verge of the abyss. No wonder then that floundering Peter reminds us of ourselves.

II

How did Peter get that way? How did he come to be sinking?

It was not because he had lost all interest in the enterprise that he had undertaken. That is, of course, the case with many that are in our churches. They are failing at the big task of being Christian because they have either never been greatly interested or have lost that interest. If these were to treat their business as they do their religion, they would be bankrupt in less than a week. If they were to treat their amusements, their bridge-playing, their golf, their dancing, in the slipshod fashion in which they treat their religion, they would be ostracized so far as these games were concerned. Nobody would have them for partners. Yet these often sadly bewail the fact that they are getting very little out of their religion. Of course not. They are putting nothing into it. Peter was failing, but it was not from lack of interest or effort.

Nor was Peter's failure born of the difficulty of his task. His task was difficult. It was difficult to the point of impossibility. But that fact does not account for his defeat. It does not account for your defeat and mine. Jesus is constantly calling us to the impossible. He calls us to be what in our own strength we cannot be. We are to be born anew. We are to become partakers of the divine nature. We are to possess the very mind that was in Christ Jesus. Then he calls upon us to accomplish tasks that in our own strength we cannot accomplish. We are to disciple the nations. We are to bring in the Kingdom of God. These are impossible tasks. "Apart from me," he tells us with engaging frankness, "you can do nothing." But with him the impossible becomes possible. "In him who strengthens me," shouts Paul, "I am able for anything." Peter's failure, therefore, was not born of his difficulties.

Why, then, did Peter fail? Here is the answer:

"He saw the wind." Peter was getting on beautifully until he decided to make a survey of the wind. He walked victoriously until he began to tabulate his problems. But when he got absorbed in the enumeration of his difficulties, at once he began to sink. When he became obsessed by his problems, the angry waves laid violent hands on him and began to drag him to the bottom of the sea. This was the case because his hindrances so completely filled his horizon that he saw nothing of what was helpful. He was so taken up by the forces that were unfriendly that he forgot those that were friendly. He became so completely wind-conscious that he ceased altogether to be Christ-conscious.

Now this is certainly one of the outstanding characteristics of our day. We are no doubt the best surveyed generation that this world has ever seen. Our age is perhaps the most problem-conscious age of all history. We see our individual problems with bewildering clearness. We also have a keen realization of our church problems, our social problems, our national problems, our international problems. These are so obvious that we cannot but see them. In addition, they are being persistently pointed out to us by pulpit and press. Naturally, these problems often so fill our horizon that we become utterly depressed and bewildered. The very keenness of our analysis of ourselves and of our situation has all but brought on paralysis. Therefore, looking only at the opposition, many of us, as Peter, are beginning to sink.

Now, this does not mean, of course, that the need of the hour is a greater blindness. Though it may seem folly to be wise, our bliss is not to come at the hands of ignorance. It is altogether to the good to face all the facts, however unpleasant they may be. Our weakness is born not so much of our facing our difficulties as of our overemphasizing of them. That always makes for weakness. There are few of us who could not walk from end to end of a fifteen-foot plank that was ten inches wide, provided that plank were lying flat on the ground. But if that same plank were made a bridge between the roofs of two 30-story skyscrapers, to walk it would be a far more difficult matter. This would be the case not because the plank had become more narrow, but because the walker had become more conscious of his difficulties. Physicians, when sick, generally are bad patients. This is the case because they are too problem-conscious. Therefore, while to know our problems is good, to be obsessed by them is a source of weakness.

It was just this problem-obsession that worked the undoing of the ten spies. These went out with Caleb and Joshua, you remember, to explore the Promised Land. The purpose of this exploration was not to determine whether or not the land could be taken. That had already been decided. It was to determine how best to accomplish the task. All of the spies undertook the exploration, it would seem, with equal enthusiasm. All found the land to be an exceedingly good land, flowing with milk and honey. All also saw the giants, the sons of Anak. But Caleb and Joshua saw these giants in the light of God. Therefore, they were in no sense terrified by them. They represented only an opportunity. "They will be bread for us," they declared with daring faith. But when the ten saw them, they so filled their horizon that they had no eye for God at all. Therefore, they were completely unmanned. "We were in our own eyes as grasshoppers," they wailed pitifully, "and so we were in their eyes." Naturally, the only contribution they could make upon their return was one of discouragement and despair. In fact, the whole enterprise of possessing the land had to wait till their generation had slipped into their coffins, because they had become too problem-conscious to be of use.

III

But the wonder of this story is that Peter changed his fear into faith and his defeat into victory. How did he do it?

He did not win by denying, or altogether ignoring, his difficulties. He did not tell himself that there really was no wind, that the waves were all a myth, that the storm had no reality except in his own mind. The fact that we overemphasize our problems does not mean that we are to shut our eyes to them altogether. When pursued by an enemy, we do not find victory by merely thrusting our heads into the sand as the ostrich is incorrectly supposed to do. Even an ostrich has too much sense for that. There is one thing, if possible, worse than a blind and stupid pessimist who sees nothing but shadows, and that is a blind and stupid optimist who sees nothing but rainbows. Peter's way out, therefore, was not to shut his eyes to the facts just because they were unpleasant.

How, then, did Peter win? When he saw that he was sinking, he frankly faced the fact. He knew that he was a disappointment to himself, a disappointment to his friends, a disappointment to his Lord. Realizing his failure, he dared to take his eyes off the wind and the waves long enough to fix them on Jesus. Fixing them on him, he prayed this simple prayer, "Lord, save me." I like the directness of it, and the brevity of it. When we are not greatly in earnest, when we neither desperately desire nor expect anything, we can pour out whole Niagaras of words before the Lord. But when the storm breaks upon us, when it is a matter of life and death, we can come to the point very quickly. "Lord, save me," cried Peter. Then what happened? "Immediately," the story says, "Jesus stretched forth his hand, and lifted him up."

Now, as old-fashioned as it may seem, I am confident that the way out for Peter is the way out for you and me. Suppose you have come this morning with a sense of defeat. You realize that you are not getting anywhere religiously. Your life seems a lean and mean affair when compared with the wealthy promises and with the wealthy personalities that you meet on the pages of the New Testament. Somehow the whole business of being a Christian has been for you little better than a failure. Your religion has been far more weight than wings. But even if this is the case, you need not despair. There is a way out. You may yet find victory. Try Peter's way. Take your gaze off your own weakness and follies and failures and fix it on Jesus. Pray his simple prayer, "Lord, save me." If you do this, a hand will surely be stretched forth to you, a hand that is mighty to save.

"But, I have prayed," some of you answer desperately. "Far into the night have I agonized in prayer. But it has got me nowhere." With Kipling's Fool, you can say, "I asked God to help me, but He didn't, He didn't." Now, we must confess that there are times when prayer seems to do no good at all. In fact, it is possible to pray in such a fashion as to do positive harm. This is the case when we focus all our attention upon our needs rather than upon Him who is able to supply our needs; when we concentrate upon the temptation from which we seek deliverance rather than upon our Deliverer. Such prayer is a source of weakness rather than of power because it enlists our imagination on the side of our temptation rather than on the side of Him from whom we seek help. Now, when there is a conflict between our will and our imagination, the psychologists tell us that the imagination always wins, and that the will goes down in defeat. Therefore, if we are going to find victory in prayer, we must fix our minds not upon our needs, but upon our victorious Lord. "Look unto me, and be ye saved." This is at once good theology and sound psychology.

That is what Jesus meant when he told the story of the embarrassed host. "Which of you shall have a friend, and shall go unto him at midnight, and say unto him, Friend, lend me three loaves; for a friend of mine in his journey is come to me, and I have nothing to set before him? and he from within shall answer and say, Trouble me not: the door is now shut, and my children are with me in bed; I cannot rise and give thee. I say unto you, Though he will not rise and give him, because he is his friend, yet because of his importunity he will rise and give him as many as he needeth." Here is a man who has an unexpected guest who has come at midnight. When this host goes to his larder to see about some food for his guest, he finds it as empty as the cupboard of Old Mother Hubbard. Then what does he do? Does he gaze with fear-filled eyes upon that emptiness while his guest has to go hungry to bed? No. He turns from his own inadequacy to the adequacy of his friend. He is so friend-conscious that he defies all difficulties, and thus receives all that he needs.

Now, just as this is the way out for the individual,

so it is for the Church. It is my firm conviction that there is no hope for the world except through the establishing of this Kingdom of God. If the Kingdom of God is not established in America, then America is doomed. If the Kingdoms of this world do not become the Kingdom of our Lord, then the world is doomed. But, how is the Kingdom of God to be established? It is my further conviction that this can only be done through the Church. This is not saying that there are not many organizations that are seeking to do good. But everyone of these that is exerting the lifting power of an ounce receives its inspiration directly or indirectly from the Church. If the Church is to establish the Kingdom, it, of course, needs to be alert and alive to the difficulties involved. But above all else, it needs to be alive to its resources, especially to those resources that are available through him who said, "All authority in heaven and in earth is given unto me." In other words, to be a victorious church, we must be a God-conscious church.

How strikingly this is illustrated by the history of the early church. Could any situation be more hopeless than the one it faced just after the Crucifixion? Its members were only a handful of scattered, discouraged, and defeated men and women who were hiding behind locked doors. They were without money, without social position, without church buildings, without schools, without any visible assets whatever. And these, whose assets were naked nothing, were confronted by stark impossibilities. But something took place that caused them to brush these impossibilities aside like so many cobwebs. In spite of seemingly irresistible foes, they went forth conquering and to conquer. How did they do it? What changed them from whipped and frightened creatures into dauntless heroes? The answer is Pentecost. And what is Pentecost? Stripped of what is merely incidental, it means just this: That these people came to realize that their Lord had come back to them in the power of the Holy Spirit. Through this experience they were made sure that henceforth he would be both with them, and within them, as their abiding Leader and Friend. It was this overwhelming consciousness of their risen Lord that made them the victorious saints that they were. This experience did for them at least four things.

First: It welded them into a brotherhood. They became united. They faced the world wearing upon their hearts the one sure badge of discipleship, love one for the other. "By this shall all men know that ye are my disciples, if ye have love one to another." By this mutual love wide chasms were bridged, and old barriers were broken down. "How these Christians love each other," said the awed and heart-hungry pagan world. And because these pagans desired to love and be loved, they were drawn into this group of brothers. A God-conscious church, a church that has experienced Pentecost, is brotherly. A brotherly church is always a growing church.

Second: This experience made these early saints shockingly aggressive. "And they called them, and commanded them not to speak at all nor teach in the name of Jesus. But Peter and John answered and said unto them, Whether it be right in the sight of God to hearken unto you more than unto God, judge ye. For we cannot but speak the things which we have seen and heard." That this was no idle boast was proven by the fact that when they were arrested again a few days later, they were sharply rebuked for their disobedience. The authorities flung the charge into their faces that though they had been commanded not to speak at all nor teach in the name of Jesus, they had filled all Jerusalem with their teachings. They were so bent on sharing that they laid almost violent hands on every passer-by to tell him of their transforming experience. Today we are timid in our witnessing. The very word "evangelism" seems to frighten us. But this is an indication of our spiritual poverty rather than of our wealth; for when the Church loses its evangelistic fervor, it is either dying or already dead. A God-conscious church is an evangelistic church.

Third: Through this experience these people became possessed of an unbelievable confidence. No difficulties, no opposition, no persecution could daunt them. They were undergirded by an abounding hopefulness. No foes could make them afraid. Publicly whipped, they departed rejoicing that they were counted worthy to suffer shame for His name. Cast into prison, they sang till their prison doors were opened and till the hearts of those who had them in charge were opened also. They were absolutely sure of final victory. "I am always confident," shouts Paul, as he faces gigantic impossibilities. And Paul's shout is the shout of this early church. They were confident because they were so sure of God. A God-conscious church is always a confident church. Its face is ever flushed with the sunshine of a dauntless optimism.

Fourth: This experience made them a powerful church. They were so powerful that they were absolutely irresistible. Age-old religions and age-old abuses vanished before them as mists vanish before the sunrise. No weapon that was formed against them could prosper. Wherever they went, the wilderness and the solitary place became glad and the desert rejoiced and blossomed as a rose. They met stern opposition, but the more they were opposed, the more they triumphed; the more they were slain, the more they lived. Why were they so mighty? The only answer is this: They were God-conscious. They had entered into the experience promised by their Lord, "Ye shall receive power, after that the Holy Spirit is come upon you."

Today, we are all but infinitely ahead of them in point of numbers and material resources. We have many large churches that are well-housed and well-organized. We have many that are possessed of wealth and culture and moral earnestness. We have the best-trained ministers in our pulpits and the best-trained teachers in our church schools of any generation since Pentecost. We have an intelligent awareness of our goals and of the problems involved in reaching them. But in spite of this, we lag. Our conquests are not vastly impressive. Though we have large and influential churches, we have too few powerful churches. What we need, therefore, is the realization that all the spiritual resources that were available for those of the long ago are available for us. We need above all else to claim their awareness of God. If we do this, we, too, shall become united, daring, confident, and powerful. Then, instead of sinking, we shall increasingly go from victory to victory.

Healing the
Syrophenician's Daughter

XV

THE GIVING OF SELF

> ***"Have mercy on me, O Lord, . . . my daughter is grievously vexed with a demon."***
>
> **MATTHEW 15: 22**

HERE IS A MOTHER WITH A SHADOW OVER HER home and a shadow over her heart. She has an afflicted daughter. Just the nature of this affliction, we are unable to say. According to the belief prevalent at that day, she is possessed by an evil spirit. But whatever her malady, it is robbing her of her opportunity. It is laying her life in ruins. But hard as it is on the daughter, it is harder still on the mother. Suffering with her child as she does, she is ready to pay any price within her power to bring her healing. Therefore, when she hears of Jesus, she hurries to him and prays this prayer: "Have mercy on me, O Lord; my daughter is grievously vexed with a demon."

This prayer is beautifully unique. This mother is not praying as we should have expected her to pray. She is not praying as we usually pray. Instead of saying, "Have mercy upon my child," she rather prays, "Have mercy upon me." Her prayer, therefore, is not an effort to stand from under, as ours so often are. She is not seeking simply to push her burden upon other shoulders, while she goes her easeful way. Her prayer is not a cheap prayer. It is costly, as real praying ever is. It costs the giving of self. She has made the burden of her daughter her very own.

Now, it is such self-giving that is required of all true prayer. We cannot really pray except at the price of self-surrender. If we refuse to surrender ourselves as we pray, then sooner or later we surrender prayer. This you have discovered for yourself, if you have ever tried to pray when there was a controversy between you and God. Did you ever try to pray when you knew there was a surrender you ought to make that you were unwilling to make? Did you ever try to pray when you kept realizing that God was pointing out a road which you ought to walk that you were refusing to walk? If you have, you know that under such circumstances one of two things always happens—either you give up yourself, or you give up prayer. Real prayer always involves surrender. God can only trust this amazing power to those that are willing to give themselves.

It is such self-giving also that is of the very essence of Christianity. "Bear ye one another's burdens," says Paul, "and so fulfill the law of Christ." What does the Apostle mean? He means, first of all, that this law of self-giving is the law by which Jesus lived. He was and is the great burden-bearer. He is constantly putting himself under our load. He takes upon himself the burden of our sin. He takes upon himself the burden of our hungers and thirsts. This he does, as he offers himself as the bread of life and as the water of life. He takes the burden of our weariness and of our restlessness, saying, "Come unto me, all ye that labor and are heavy-laden, and I will give you rest." He is constantly offering himself as the bearer of our burdens. This sums up the whole meaning of his life from the manger to the cross.

But, not only is this the law by which Jesus lived, it is also the law by which he expects us to live. What he did and does, he counts upon us to do also. We are to have his mind, his disposition, his way of looking at things. We are to have his way of doing things. We are to give ourselves for the good of others, even as he. "If he laid down his life for us, we ought also to lay down our lives for the brethren." It was in this spirit that the early Christians lived. It is in this spirit that we are to live. We cannot be truly Christian in any other way.

"Must Jesus bear the cross alone,
And all the world go free?
No, there's a cross for every one,
And there's a cross for me!"

It is only as we bear one another's burdens that we can fulfill the law of Christ.

II

Why does Jesus make self-giving the law of life for you and me?

He does not do so because he looks upon sacrifice as an end in itself. To afflict ourselves, to cause ourselves needless suffering, is not in itself a virtue. I read some time ago of a girl who sought to atone for some wrong that she had done by beating up glass and putting in her shoes. But God was not honored by her thus making herself a cripple. Suffering is never an end in itself. Simon Stylites standing for years upon his pedestal certainly practiced self-sacrifice, but I am not at all sure that by so doing he rendered the slightest benefit either to himself or to anyone else. Self-giving, even to the last limit, is not necessarily a good. "If I bestow all my goods to feed the poor, and give my body to be burned, and have not love, it profiteth me nothing."

If sacrifice in the sense of surrendering something of value were an end in itself, then those who are farthest from wishing to make any sacrifice at all would be the most enriched. This is the case because nobody gives up quite so much as those who are most determined to give nothing. When the Prodigal went into the far country, he certainly had no thought of making any sacrifice. But in spite of this fact, he found the adventure to be very costly. It cost him the companionship of his father. It cost him gnawing hungers and burning thirsts. It cost him his usefulness. It cost him everything. He literally spent all that he had. It is true, therefore, that none surrender so much as those who are most bent on surrendering nothing at all.

Why, then, I repeat, does Jesus ask you and me to make self-giving the law of our lives?

1. He does so because he knows that it is only as we give ourselves that we can achieve our highest usefulness. But this self-giving, to be of supreme value, must have at least two characteristics. First, it must be voluntary. It is only thus that it is shot through with the spirit of the cross. We sometimes speak of certain burdens as our cross, when those burdens are thrust upon us. We have to bear them whether we are willing to do so or not. But we can only count that as our cross that we bear of our own choice. That was the case with the cross of Jesus. He did not have to bear it. When he spoke of the giving up of his life on the cross, he said, "No man taketh it from me, but I lay it down of myself."

Not only must the burdens we bear be borne voluntarily, they must be borne from a worthy motive. Jesus never looked upon any form of suffering as an end in itself, not even that of the cross. Why did he put himself under the burdens of others, even to the point of going to Calvary for them? It was for the joy that was set before him that he endured the cross, despising the shame. This joy was not the joy of suffering, but the joy of winning the world through suffering. He suffered because of the conviction that after he was lifted up, he would draw all men unto himself. It was through his self-giving on the cross that he expected to attain his highest usefulness. And all the subsequent centuries bear witness to the fact that his expectation was well founded.

Now we, too, can only serve in a superlative way at the price of life laid down. This, of course, does not mean that we cannot render many helpful services at a lesser cost. We can and do give and serve in such fashion as to win high commendation without going to such extremes. But, in spite of all that, it still remains true that we never accomplish our best, never realize our highest, except at the price of the giving of self. This is true in every department of human endeavor.

Take literature and art, for instance. There are comparatively few books that are of permanent value. Many are timely, but it is an exceedingly rare book that is also timeless. What are the books that live? Milton describes such when he declares, "Books are not absolutely dead things; they are the precious lifeblood of a master spirit, embalmed and treasured up on purposes to a life beyond life." That is, the book that lives is the costly book. It is one into which the author has poured his lifeblood. He has written it at the price of life laid down.

This is equally true in the realm of art. No great picture is painted except at a great price. That is the lesson of that oft-told story of the artist whose pictures had in them an inimitable coloring, a bewildering crimson, that caused them to cast a spell upon every beholder. Other artists, charmed by their beauty and power, sought to learn the secret, only to give up in despair. At last, the great painter died, and everyone thought that his secret had perished with him. But when they were preparing him for burial, they discovered above his heart an old half-healed wound. Then they understood. As this artist had painted, he had dipped his brush into his own heart's blood. That is, his painting was a parting with life. His work was done, as all really superlative work is done, at the price of life laid down.

This is equally true of all high service. This week, a man who gave away more in terms of money, I dare say, than any other that ever lived, passed to his reward. His gifts amounted to more than five hundred and thirty millions of dollars. Not only did he give lavishly, but he gave wisely. His money will doubtless be serving humanity centuries from now. Yet, strange as it may seem, the world will still remember the meager gift of a certain widow of the long ago, will still grow tender-hearted over it, when the gifts of this multimillionaire have been forgotten. Why is this the case? What comparison is there between five hundred and thirty millions of dollars and two mites? Surely none in quantity. The gift of Mr. Rockefeller was almost infinitely greater than that of the widow. But there was a quality about the gift of this woman that does not belong to the gift of the billionaire. He gave out of his superfluity, as the scriptures would say, just as those other rich men of the long ago. But she gave out of her want. She gave her all. Her gift was crimsoned with the blood of sacrifice. And we never give our best except at this high price.

As with giving, so it is with all service that is superlative.

> "I sometimes think that never blows so red
> The rose, as where some buried Caesar bled."

There is a sense in which this is profoundly and literally true. Flowers of Christlike character certainly grow in their richest profusion only where the soil has been fertilized by the lives of those who have given themselves. This is true of the homes where boys and girls have the best opportunities of growing into fine men and women. This is true of every church, every community, where the fields grow golden with harvests of transformed lives.

Some years ago, a missionary went to preach in an obscure Chinese village. When the people gathered about him, he began to tell them about Jesus. He told how he went about doing good, how he suffered in the sufferings of others, how he made every man's burden his burden. As he spoke, their faces took on a new radiance and their eyes became bright with understanding. "We know him," they said eagerly. "He has been here. He used to live among us. He is buried in our cemetery." The missionary was amazed and bewildered. "Where is he buried?" he asked. And they led him to a well-kept grave whose headstone bore the name of a Christian physician whom the outside world had forgotten. This man had flung himself away on those obscure villagers. And though the big world had forgotten him, this soil that he had fertilized by his life had become colorful with human flowers.

2. Then Jesus urges us to the giving of self, not only because this is the way to our highest usefulness, but also to our highest self-realization. When we talk about self-giving, the thought that persistently haunts so many is this: Such self-giving is well enough for those who are on the receiving end; but how about the givers, where do they come in? It is fine, of course, to have somebody to sacrifice for you, somebody willing to part with life on your behalf. There is often no measuring the value of such sacrifices to those in whose behalf they are made. But how about those that have to make them? Surely they are doing more than their part, and are, therefore, allowing themselves to be cheated.

But instead of this being the case, the very opposite is true. If giving self for others enriches the receiver, it enriches the giver even more. Much is being said today about personality. We once thought that personality was purely a matter of gift. We either had it or did not. But we are learning now that personality is something that we can develop. How are we to go about it? By self-giving. One of our leading psychologists tells us that our personalities grow just in proportion to our ability to do things with and for others. That is, other things being equal, the greater the abandon with which we give ourselves away, the greater and richer our personalities become.

Who is it, then, that lives most abundantly? It is the one who flings his life away in the service of others. A few years ago a young Japanese student left our shores for his home with the sentence of death passed upon him. His physicians told him that he had only one lung and, therefore, could live but a brief while. He decided, since this was the case, to make the short hour that was left him count for the most possible. He therefore buried himself in one of the worst slums in his native land. He gave himself so lavishly that the tides of spiritual power that flowed into him made death impossible. He is living still—creatively and mightily. In fact, this man with his physical handicap is perhaps the most powerful and influential Christian in the world today. To fulfill the law of Christ, then, by self-giving is at once the way of highest usefulness and of highest self-realization.

III

Look at what such self-giving did in this story before you. "Have mercy upon me," prayed this sorrowing mother; "my daughter is grievously vexed with a demon." What was the worth of that prayer to the one on whose behalf it was offered? Was it of any value at all? I was reading recently a book on prayer written by one of our most earnest young ministers. Much in the book was at once sane, scriptural, and helpful. But with youthful arrogance he threw intercessory prayer completely into the discard. To his way of thinking, it is utterly useless for one man to pray for another. But to take such a position is to make nonsense of much that is most beautiful and helpful in both the Old and the New Testaments. Jesus himself offered such prayers again and again. Paul never wrote but one letter, the one to the backslidden church at Galatia, without asking an interest in the prayers of those to whom he wrote. He believed that the humblest of the saints could thus anoint his lips with grace and power. And such has been the faith of the saints throughout the centuries.

That there are mysteries connected with intercessory prayer, I am not denying. Nor am I undertaking at this time in any way to clarify these mysteries. But what I do affirm is this, that we are taught throughout the Bible to pray one for another. "God forbid that I should sin against the Lord," said the prophet of the long ago, "by ceasing to pray for you." Such praying does make it possible for God to do for us what otherwise He cannot do. It was so here. It was through this woman's prayer that healing came to her daughter. By her prayer, she took her afflicted child in her arms and fairly laid her upon the lap of God. So saintly mothers have done countless numbers of times. We remember such this day with tenderness, for many reasons; but for none more than this, the prayers they offered on our behalf.

But, though this self-giving prayer brought help and healing to the daughter, that was but the lesser of its benefits. It did even more for the mother. However much, therefore, this mother gave, it was little in comparison with what she received. I know of nothing in the entire experience of our Lord that brought him greater joy, nothing over which he showed a greater enthusiasm, than over the persistent, faith-prompted prayer of this mother. He who had at first seemed to meet her request with flat refusal, turned at last to say, "O woman, great is thy faith. Be it unto thee, even as thou wilt." Thus while her prayer brought a blessing to her child, it brought an even greater blessing to herself.

It is ever the case. It was by such self-giving that our Lord won his crown. "Have this mind in you, which was also in Christ Jesus: who, existing in the form of God, counted not the being on an equality with God a thing to be grasped, but emptied himself, taking the form of a servant, being made in the likeness of men; and being found in fashion as a man, he humbled himself, becoming obedient even unto death, yea, the death of the cross. Wherefore also God highly exalted him, and gave unto him the name which is above every name; that in the name of Jesus every knee should bow, of things in heaven and things on earth and things under the earth, and that every tongue should confess that Jesus Christ is Lord, to the glory of God the Father." Thus, according to St. Paul, Jesus climbed to the highest heights because he was willing to stoop to the lowest depths of humiliation and shame.

There is a story that, once on a time, a certain Chinese King ordered his chief minister to make a bell that would ring with a note of flawless sweetness. This King put all the treasures of his vast kingdom at the disposal of his minister. Therefore, having received such a commission, the minister went out and gathered together the choicest silver and gold of the realm. He flung this into a great caldron, melted it, and cast his wonderful bell. But when it was swung in the tower and the King and his subjects were gathered to hear it ring, they were disappointed. While there was music, it was soulless and metallic, with no note of tenderness. It was, therefore, as jarring as instruments played out of tune.

The King, therefore, ordered that the bell be recast. This was done. Again it was swung in the tower and again the King and his subjects gathered to hear the music. But again they were disappointed. There was still that soulless tone that jarred rather than soothed and healed. Then the King became angry. He summoned his minister and commanded him to cast the bell a third time. He further warned him that, unless it should ring with flawless sweetness this time, his life would be the forfeit. That evening, therefore, the minister went home with a heavy heart. He knew not what to do. When his wife and daughter pressed him for the reason for his sadness, he told the story of his pathetic plight.

Now, it so happened that this daughter loved her father with unusual devotion. When, therefore, she heard his story, it almost broke her heart. She resolved that at all cost she would do something to help. Therefore, that night, when all slept, she slipped out of the house and down the street to where the Wise Man lived. She told him her story and asked how the bell might be made to ring with a note of flawless sweetness. With deep solemnity, the Wise Man gave the answer: "If the bell is to ring with flawless sweetness, it must have in it something more than silver and gold. With the metal, there must be mingled the blood of a devoted heart."

Pondering this truth in her mind, the girl went home again. She had resolved what to do. Therefore, the next day when the metal was seething and hissing over the hot fires, before any hands could stay her, she threw herself into the boiling caldron. With the silver and gold was mingled the blood of her devoted heart. Then the bell was cast once more. Once more, it was hung in the tower. Once more, the King and the people gathered to hear it ring. And what a change had taken place! This time, as they listened, tears wet every face, every heart grew soft and tender, for such heavenly music had never been heard before. And our lives are like that—yours and mine. They never reach their best, they never attain their highest possible sweetness and beauty, except at the price of utter self-giving.

The Healing of Bartimaeus

XVI

ON THE SIDE LINE

"Blind Bartimaeus, the son of Timaeus, sat by the highway side begging."

MARK 10: 46

HERE IS A PATHETIC CHARACTER. HE IS A MAN that nobody envied. A few perhaps pitied him, and many despised him. He is a blot upon the landscape, a bit of human wreckage that tends to raise in our minds questions of the goodness and love of God. Of course the fact that he is what he is, is not altogether his fault. He is far more sinned against than sinning. Most of the blame rests upon the society of his day that made no provision for men of his kind. But regardless of who is at fault, Bartimaeus himself is a mere ragged pocket that calamity has turned inside out and emptied of everything of worth.

I

What is wrong with this man?

1. He is blind. That is always a tragic loss. He has been born blind. He has never been privileged to

witness the miracle of a sunrise nor the blazing glory of a sunset. He has never looked into the blue of the sky, nor into the face of a little child. But this fact need not have resulted in utter disaster. Many have lived in the light in spite of their blindness. John Milton was blind, yet he was not for that reason a creature of the dark. He was rather a child of the flaming dawn. He was speaking out of his own experience when he sang:

> "He that has light within his own clear breast
> May sit in the center and enjoy bright day:
> But he that hides a dark soul and foul thoughts
> Benighted walks under the midday sun;
> Himself is his own dungeon."

2. Not only is Bartimaeus blind, but he is also poor. He is so poor that he is compelled to wear the threadbare and ragged castoff garments of others. He is so poor that he has often to suffer the pangs of hunger. Such poverty is a tragic something. It tends always to suppress our noble rage and freeze the genial current of the soul. But even poverty need not prove fatal. Many have, through high faith and courage, changed their poverty into spiritual plenty and their want into wealth.

3. The supreme tragedy of Bartimaeus consists in what he has allowed his blindness and poverty to do for him. They have put him on the side line. He is out of the game. He is not one of the world's workers. He is an idler, a parasite, a blind mouth,

living off of the work of others. Thus compelled to live on charity, his morale has been destroyed. He has lost his self-respect. He is not only a beggar, but content to be one. He has reached the conclusion that the world owes him a living. He lives only for himself. Every footfall that he hears along the highway sets him to asking this one question: "What can I get out of this passerby?" He has become so utterly blind spiritually that he thinks the big business of life is not giving, but getting.

II

Now, this type of spiritual blindness has lived through the centuries.

We meet it in the long ago. Here, for instance, is a story out of Mythology: When Achilles was born, his mother went to consult the Oracle of Delphi as to his future. The Oracle told her that her son would either live a long life of inglorious ease, or a short life of battle and victory. With the blindness of Bartimaeus, she chose for her son the long life of uselessness. Therefore, she dressed him up like a girl and put him out on an island where nobody lived but girls, where he seemed destined to live and die in idle worthlessness.

By and by, however, the Greeks went to war against the Trojans. For a long time they fought about her walls in vain. Then, they went to consult the Oracle of Delphi as to how they could win the victory. The

Oracle told them that they could never win except Achilles fought with them and for them. But nobody knew where Achilles was. But that wily detective among the Greeks, Ulysses by name, undertook to find him. He traveled over all lands until he came to that island where nobody lived but girls. Then, disguised as a peddler, he went among them to sell his wares. They bought eagerly, all except one. At last he lifted from among his feminine trinkets a suit of armor and a sword. At sight of that this girl sprang forward eagerly, fitted on the armor and began to wield the sword. Thus Ulysses recognized Achilles, the hero. He chose that with which he might serve instead of that with which he might be served. But his escape was not by virtue of, but in spite of, the blindness of his mother.

But this blindness is not simply of yesterday, it is also of today. In a recent issue of the *American Magazine,* there was an article by a young man of more than ordinary intelligence. He was propounding this question: "Why should I be honest?" He shut out all religious and idealistic answers by saying: "I do not wish to be great, I only desire to be comfortable." But no man could write after this fashion who was not stone-blind spiritually, blind to the fact that he himself is something more than a mere animal. A pig may be comfortable if he has plenty to eat, even if his swill is stolen. The herd of hogs that the prodigal fed were comfortable enough, but their fare did not suffice for the prodigal himself. He was tormented by dreams that made his soul sick and restless. Of course he might have disregarded this restlessness till he had become possessed of a certain content. But this would have been the contentment of death rather than of life. The trouble with this young man is just plain blindness.

Too often we meet this same type of blindness in the world of business. A bright young chap said the other day: "I'm not in business for my health; I'm in it strictly for the money I can make out of it." And, sad to say, there are those who are not shocked by such a devilish declaration. These rather nod their heads sagely as if he were talking the language of wisdom. Recently a gentleman gave me a letter written by a man who claimed to be a churchman. This man was railing against the Federal Council of Churches because this organization had objected to the profit motive in business. This good brother was outraged, and was threatening to wreck the Church by withdrawing from it altogether. Of course there are certain types of so-called business with which no one but selfish getters will have anything to do. Take the liquor business, for example. What is the motive of the liquor dealer? Crass and utter selfishness. He is out for number one. He is out to get all he can, even at the price of blood and tears. Gambling is very prevalent among us today. What is the motive of the gambler? He is seeking to get something for nothing. At his best, he is a parasite; at his worst, he is a fool.

But when we come to the realm of legitimate business we expect something better. In many instances I am happy to say that our expectations are not disappointed. Why should not this be the case? Why, in all common sense, should the motive of the business man be less high than that of other workers? Suppose I should announce from this pulpit: "I am not preaching for my health. I am preaching strictly for the money." Every one of you would despise me. Suppose the physician should stand in the presence of pain and death and never undertake to aid unless he saw the glint of a dollar. You would look upon him with contempt. Every man, regardless of the nature of his work, must recognize the fact that he is not come to be ministered unto, but to minister. The business man who fails to realize this is blind, and such blindness is not only bad morals, but bad business.

III

But one day blind Bartimaeus was utterly changed. He ceased merely to exist and began to live. How did this come about? Of course the first move was made by Jesus. That is always the case. He ever seeks us before we seek him. His help here, too, was brought, in part, as almost always, through human hands. Look at the steps by which Bartimaeus came into the light.

It is quite evident that this beggar had heard of

Jesus before his encounter with him here on the highway. One day, doubtless, there had passed along his road a man who was more kindly than the average. After he had dropped a penny into the clutching fingers of the beggar, he looked at him with a mingling of loathing and pity. Then, he asked him a question: "Bartimaeus, why don't you get well? Why don't you quit this sordid business of begging and do something worthwhile?" "Get well," he answered with pained amazement, not unmixed with anger. "Get well? How can I get well? Don't you know I was born blind? My father was blind before me. I have always been like this, and there is no chance of my ever being different. Why do you mock me by a question like that?"

"I did not mean to mock you," came the kindly answer. "You can get well if you will. Is it possible that you have not heard of the amazing Prophet that has come among us? He has power beyond the human. I have known him to heal the sick by a word. I have known him to touch lepers into purity. He has even made the roses of life to bloom upon the frozen cheeks of death. I tell you, there is a chance for you." And the beggar's face becomes one lean wistfulness. "What is his name?" he inquires eagerly. "His name is Jesus, and he is of the house and lineage of David," is the answer. "Jesus, the Son of David!" the beggar murmurs to himself. "Jesus, the Son of David. Well, if he ever comes my way, I'm going to ask him."

During the days that followed, Bartimaeus was filled with a growing discontent. The meanness of his lot was increasingly distasteful. But along with his discontent was a strange, new expectancy. He did not know what day Jesus might come his way. Every morning, though he awoke in the dark, he was thrilled by the thought that something big might come into his life that day. "With a Prophet like Jesus abroad in the land, anything wonderful is likely to happen," he told himself. And he was right. We are not half as expectant as we should be. There is nothing too good to take place in the meanest of our lives when a Christ like ours is so eager and so near.

Then, at last his great day dawned. There was the tramp of many feet along the highway. Something was happening that stirred his heart and set his soul to dreaming. Could it be Jesus? He was not quite sure. He needed somebody to interpret to him these movements along the highway. That is often the case with ourselves. Samuel needed the wise old prophet to explain to him that the voice that called him in such a human fashion was after all God's voice. What is the meaning of the stirring of your own heart? Why is it that sometimes, in the most unlikely situations, at a cocktail party, or down at the Sunday show, you are suddenly strangely disgusted and sick of it all? What does it mean that there are times that you feel that you would give your very life to break with sin, and be what you ought to be? O heart, it means for you what it meant for Bartimaeus in the long ago. It means that Jesus is passing your way. To all he comes, though sometimes we fail to have ears to hear and eyes to see.

When Bartimaeus heard that Jesus was passing, what effect did it have on him? Did he pursue his beggar's trade as if nothing big and worthwhile were afoot? No. The great news electrified him. It set his sluggish heart to pounding as if it would leap from his bosom. Of course some of us can hear such news without the tremor of an eyelash. But not so, this beggar. It thrilled him. Not only so, it set him to praying. His was not a long prayer, but it was intense and to the point. When we neither desire anything nor expect anything, we can pour out torrents of words in the form of prayer; but when the sword of a great need has pierced our hearts, then we come to the point. So it was with this blind beggar. "Jesus, thou Son of David, have mercy on me." Bartimaeus put all his knowledge and all his soul into that prayer. The man who told him that Jesus was passing called him "Jesus of Nazareth"; but this beggar recognizes him as the Messiah and calls him the Son of David.

But, there were those present who were shocked by the loud outcries of this beggar. They felt that such tumultuous praying was unseemly. They believed in dignity. They were convinced that even prayers to be effective ought to be built on the Gothic style of architecture. Of course real dignity is quite worthwhile.

But there is a type of dignity that has been well described as "a pose of the body to conceal the defects of the soul." Such is the case with those who are more concerned with being dignified than with being helpful. They ordered this beggar to keep quiet. We never do that, in so many words, but sometimes we silence the supplicants just as effectively by our knowing looks, by our smugness, by our lack of sympathy.

But Bartimaeus was not to be silenced. He was a stout-hearted man. He was bent on winning through to daylight. Seeing the crowd was against him, he only shouted the louder. The greater the opposition, the more determined and desperate became his efforts. I feel like reaching a hand across the centuries to congratulate him. And above the hot words of those who would stop him, Jesus heard his cry. Of course we are not to understand that it was the prayer of this beggar that made Jesus willing to help him. But it was through this prayer that Bartimaeus opened the door of his heart and invited Jesus to enter. And his invitation was not in vain. Jesus stopped and commanded him to be called. And those who have just been his foes are now his friends. Those who a moment ago were getting in his way and commanding him to silence now hurry to his side eager to help. "Courage," they say; "He is calling for thee."

What a thrill this must have brought to Bartimaeus! Nobody had ever wanted him before. Nobody had ever called him. But now this is the word: "Page

Bartimaeus." Who wants him? Jesus wants him. He is eagerly waiting for his approach. And that is my message to you. He is calling for thee. He knows where you sit. He knows the longings of your heart. He knows how dismally and how desperately you have failed. He knows how marvelously you may succeed. He knows all your possibilities. He is looking wistfully at you this moment, singling you out from all that have lived and from all that do live. He knows that he can do something for you that nobody else can do, and that you can do something for him that nobody else can do. "He is calling for thee."

And what did Bartimaeus do, when he heard that good news? He threw aside his beggar's cloak and came at once to Jesus. This man was putting first things first. He would not cling to anything that would hinder him. It was not a sin to wear that old threadbare coat, but it was in the way. Therefore, he parted with it at once. If you come, you must fling away all known sin. You must go even further than that. You must throw away those practices that are not in themselves sinful, but that hinder your usefulness. "Therefore, laying aside every weight and the sin that doth so easily beset us, let us run with patience the race that is set before us." That was what this beggar did. Let us be wise with his wisdom!

Now, because Bartimaeus was willing to give up all for Jesus, Jesus was willing and eager to give all to him. "The eyes of the Lord run to and fro throughout the whole earth, to show himself strong in behalf" of such surrendered souls. It is to these that Jesus can say, "Son, thou art ever with me, and all that I have is thine." Bartimaeus had little enough to give up, a beggar's life in darkness, and a beggar's ragged coat. But, in exchange for these worthless nothings, Jesus put the key of heaven into his hand. "What wilt thou that I should do unto thee?" he asked. "Lord," came the answer, "that my eyes may be opened." And with that the day dawned and the shadows fled away.

IV

What was the outcome? Bartimaeus was not only healed of his physical blindness, but he was healed of his spiritual blindness as well. In fact, this is the supreme miracle of the story. If Bartimaeus had continued in the dark physically his experience would have lost little of its winsome wonder. Having found Jesus, he got off the side line. He got into the game. He began to follow Him whose road always leads where battles for righteousness are to be fought, and where wounds are to be healed. Thus following, he experienced for the first time the high luxury of usefulness and the sweet joy of being wanted. Paul, writing to certain friends of his, said: "Whenever I think of you, I thank God." So, Luke tells us, it came to be with this one-time beggar. When folks thought of him, they thought of God and gave Him thanks.

I heard Dr. Luccock say that while he was in Europe he visited two rooms that impressed him deeply. One was the Hall of Mirrors. In this hall, he could see nothing but repeated images of himself. In one nook he could see himself seven times at a single glance. But in a certain Swiss village, he went into another room that was so full of windows that he called it the "Room of Windows." Here he could not see one single image of himself. But his compensation for this loss was the fact that he could look out and see the wide world. Before Jesus came, Bartimaeus lived in the Hall of Mirrors where he saw nobody but himself. But through this experience he entered "the house of windows" where he no longer saw himself, but Jesus and a needy world. God grant that a like experience may come to ourselves.